Learning Beyond the Objective in Primary Education

Learning Beyond the Objective in Primary Education explores an existential perspective for pedagogy proposed in response to the current technocratic paradigm of education prevalent in many countries worldwide. This new perspective is termed 'Bildung's Repetition.' The book seeks to encourage policy makers and educational practitioners to consider the impact of education on children, *over and above* the meeting of set targets and objectives.

Located in a philosophical framework, this book considers how children might learn authentically in the light of their own personal contingency. A series of case studies reflecting the effectiveness of this perspective through the curriculum is provided, each illustrating how 'Bildung's Repetition' allows for personalised meaningful learning within current structures. Recommendations for practice are provided, encouraging all stakeholders in education to consider the value of this perspective, and effect a 'ten-degree shift' within educational thought.

This unique book fuses theory with practice, and will be of great interest to academics, researchers and students in the fields of primary education and teacher training. It will also be of interest to school leaders and practicing teachers.

Ruth Wills is a part-time teacher in a primary school, an associate lecturer at Liverpool Hope University and a foster carer.

Learning Beyond the Objective in Primary Education

Philosophical Perspectives from Theory and Practice

Ruth Wills

Routledge
Taylor & Francis Group

LONDON AND NEW YORK

First published 2020
by Routledge
2 Park Square, Milton Park, Abingdon, Oxon OX14 4RN

and by Routledge
52 Vanderbilt Avenue, New York, NY 10017

Routledge is an imprint of the Taylor & Francis Group, an informa business

First issued in paperback 2021

British Library Cataloguing-in-Publication Data
A catalogue record for this book is available from the British Library

Library of Congress Cataloging-in-Publication Data
Names: Wills, Ruth, author.
Title: Learning beyond the objective in primary education: philosophical perspectives from theory and practice / Ruth Wills.
Description: Abingdon, Oxon; New York, NY: Routledge, 2020. | Includes bibliographic references.
Identifiers: LCCN 2019014884 (print) | LCCN 2019021806 (ebook) | ISBN 9780429201233 (E-book) | ISBN 9780367192365 (hardback) | ISBN 9780429201233 (ebook)
Subjects: LCSH: Education, Primary—Aims and objectives. | Education, Primary—Philosophy. | Transformative learning. | Education and state.
Classification: LCC LB1513 (ebook) | LCC LB1513 .W55 2020 (print) | DDC 372/.011—dc23
LC record available at https://lccn.loc.gov/2019014884

ISBN: 978-0-367-19236-5 (hbk)
ISBN: 978-1-03-209194-5 (pbk)
ISBN: 978-0-429-20123-3 (ebk)

Typeset in Times New Roman
by codeMantra

Contents

Acknowledgements

This book represents a very long journey of teaching, thinking and writing. I have been guided along the way by many people, more than mentioned here.

But first I thank all the staff and pupils, past and present, of St. Mary's Catholic Primary School. Thank you for the all encouragement and support you have given and for allowing me the space to explore my ideas.

Thank you to Dr. Marie Morgan – my PhD supervisor, mentor and friend – for providing insight, wisdom and inspiration through my studies, and for all at the University of Winchester who came alongside me during my 6 years of research.

Thanks go to my friends and colleagues in the International Association for Children's Spirituality – for the opportunities, conversations, good times and not least the singing.

Also, to my new colleagues in the Department of Early Childhood at Liverpool Hope University – thank you for welcoming me.

Posthumously, I would like to thank Professor Canon John Atherton, for showing an interest in my work and for connecting me with a wider network.

I would also like to thank Emilie Coin and Will Bateman at Routledge, for seeing the potential in this project and bringing it into reality.

Finally, to my family, Daniel and Elvis – I love you.

Introduction

Background

The inspiration for this book came in a 'moment' during a seminar at my university. As part of my role as a visiting fellow, I gave a presentation that reflected the some of the theoretical material from my PhD thesis, including the themes of authenticity and transformation in the classroom. Aware of the highs and lows of teaching life, the aim of the session was to encourage the participants to consider how an existential dimension in learning might be recognised, so to consider a nuanced pedagogical perspective. By the term existential, I refer to a form of education that allows students to understand the meaning and purpose of their existence (Webster 2004: 9).

Drawing on case studies from my own school experience, I proposed that when the teacher allows the lesson to enable learners to embrace reflection within the learning environment or setting, using the set 'learning objective' as a platform for personal development as well as an end result, the lesson becomes more than a box to tick, but an opportunity for transformation. I suggested that teachers might consider the learning that happens 'beyond the objective,' that is, to see the potential in education for personal development. This stirred a response. In a moment of enthusiasm, the questions that followed the presentation homed in on this particular statement, leading me to consider more fully what the rationale behind the statement was. Following the seminar, I also considered how this might become manifest in real educational life.

To implement this idea certainly is not easy, given the myriad of responsibilities that teachers have to undertake. It is also risky as it questions the roles of both teacher and learner, and considers the possible groundlessness of an authoritative other. However, as will be outlined later, when the teacher creates the condition for authentic learning, the authority of the 'other' is not negated but rather suspended, creating space for reflection, deeper thinking and ultimately, change. It is proposed here that this perspective can become embedded into the culture of the classroom for long-lasting learning.

The objective

So, what is a learning objective? In a Primary School in England, planning and assessment are currently framed by a National Curriculum prescribed by the Department for Education.[1] Based on statutory Programmes of Study for each subject, learners in every lesson are required to achieve a set 'learning objective' (LO). This objective indicates to the students what 'we are learning to' do (sometimes recognised in the child-friendly acronym WALT). Success criteria, that is, 'what I am looking for' (WILF) indicate how far each learner has come in respect of meeting the objective, and evidence in books or data recorded in a digital format indicate what progress has been made.

The 'learning objective' has been a feature of English schools for several years. A 2004 document,[2] which outlines the value of assessment, explains that a lesson's learning objective provides a 'shared understanding of what is to be learned.' The objective is presented at the beginning of a lesson, written on the (white) board, posted on the wall or written/stuck in books. Throughout and following lessons, ongoing oral and written feedback highlights to the learners how far they have been successful in meeting the learning objective, and this formative assessment inspires future planning and progress.

Currently in England, specific learning objectives are sometimes devised by class teachers who draw the objectives from local curriculum frameworks. These are in turn drawn from the Programmes of Study for each subject published by the Department for Education. Other schools frame their lessons according to externally agreed learning objectives listed on digital data processing programmes.[3] For example, a learning objective for older children in history is: *we are learning to evaluate sources to understand an historical event.* An example of a learning objective for younger children in art is: *we are learning to plan, design and create a model from observation.* Progress is then measured against these objectives. Assessment indicates whether children are *developing, secure* or have grasped the objective in *greater depth.* Through each school's tracking system, individual progress is made evident, indicating pupil's needs and informing possible interventions.

In theory, teaching to objectives should enable teachers and learners to stay focused in lessons and recognise what has been achieved.

Nevertheless, prioritising the learning objective can also be problematic, not least for the creative and critical teacher who might feel that lessons are limited by closed-ended objectives. For example, in one lesson on which I was observed, specific focus on the learning objective 'we are learning to explore texture in music' set both the children and I up to fail. When asked by the observer 'what are you learning?' the children all replied 'about the Romans.' Of course, the children were composing music about the Romans, through which they explored how different layers of sound (texture) can create effects. Yet their misunderstanding of the learning objective supposedly meant that the children did not achieve.

Nevertheless, when considering the value of the lesson from a different perspective, that is in terms of holistic learning, the children *did* achieve. A number of educational moments took place, which I suggest, were equally important to them as learning individuals and as a collective.

- Children worked collaboratively in groups, discussing and evaluating their ideas.
- They learnt to share and take turns.
- They allowed their imaginations to take them to the world of Ancient Rome.
- They were expressive in their creativity and supportive in their evaluation of their own and other's work.

In the light of this, I propose that being a teacher involves *much more* than steering learners towards the meeting of objectives. I posit that a dimension of learning does exist which is 'beyond the objective.' But not only does the primary school experience involve the social, creative and spiritual aspects of learning illustrated in the example above; there is, I suggest, an existential dimension which should be recognised and valued. This dimension concerns learning that has a personal and long-lasting impact on children, is meaningful to them and in some ways might effect change.

In this book then, I propose that such a dimension encourages teachers and school leaders to think again about what 'education' means. In order to illustrate my proposition, I will draw on significant moments from within the range of school experiences I have enjoyed, both in the UK and in Europe. Whilst locating my ideas within a philosophical framework, I will refer to significant experiences that have actually happened in school and consider ways in which teachers and teacher educators might create the conditions for such experiences in their own schools and classrooms. Furthermore, I will offer recommendations to Governments and policy makers, calling for a change in perspective and a 'ten-degree shift' in practice.

It might be argued that an existential educational perspective is best proposed as antithetical to what might be described as the performativity culture within a number of educational structures, not only in the UK but on a wider international stage.[4] Of course, being located in England, my first port of call in highlighting issues and providing examples will be my own context. However, I maintain that equivalent issues are evident on a much wider scale, and I suggest that the ideas presented in this book will have significance for practitioners in other global situations who feel similarly uncomfortable with the values of an achievement-driven paradigm.

The opening chapter includes a summary of global expectations for schools and educational success. The ongoing discussion then seeks to negotiate an existential perspective within, rather than at a tangent to, the existing paradigm which it must be recognised might take many years to overturn. This involves the proposal of a dialectical relationship between the current context and the existence of the learner using philosophical ideas and a nuanced movement of learning. Furthermore, the philosophical ideas must be workable in practice. Therefore, later material includes case studies representing the existential value of curriculum areas such as history, geography, creative writing, mathematics and the arts. Initiatives such as Forest Schools and eco-education are also given attention. In conclusion, it is proposed how such a perspective might influence pedagogy, so to place higher priority on the Being[5] of learners for an approach to education that is authentic and transformational.

Notes

1 www.gov.uk/dfe/nationalcurriculum accessed 22/11/2018.
2 https://www.lancsngfl.ac.uk/curriculum/assessment/download/file/04%20 Day%20to%20Day%20Ass%20Strategies.pdf accessed 22/11/2018.
3 An example of a digital data processing programme is Classroom Monitor: www.classroommonitor.co.uk.
4 The performativity culture is described in Chapter 1.
5 This is an Heideggerian concept which is explored in Chapter 2.

Reference

Webster, R.S. (2004), 'An existential framework of spirituality,' in *International Journal of Children's Spirituality*, 9, No. 1. 7–19.

1   An overview of educational policy and practice

Setting the scene: England

Earlier this decade, a new National Curriculum for England was published. When one considers its initial statement of aims, it is clear that this framework is knowledge based. The document that outlines the curriculum declares that participants in education will be introduced to 'the best that has been thought and said.'[1] Learners will gain 'knowledge, understanding and skills' and are expected to develop competence and achieve (5). Since the National Curriculum became statutory in 2014, school leaders and teachers have needed to shift the emphasis in their teaching methods somewhat, with experiential learning, for example, taking a back seat. This has become evidenced now by some classrooms having children's desks placed in rows. Practitioners have been required to develop a new set of information and skills in order to meet the prescribed criteria for learning; thus, children in primary schools now need to know the 'language about language,' such as the widely debated 'fronted adverbial'[2] as well as understand more complex mathematical concepts including algebra and statistics (138; 141).

Most notably, teachers have been required to prepare primary school leavers for more rigorous tests. Subsequently, the main focus in the final year at least is attaining predetermined academic outcomes for learning, with other year groups having to negotiate more knowledge-based activities. For example, in science topics the statutory requirements expect children to observe, describe, label and compare, rather than experiment, predict and create. In music, the rhetoric of history, evaluation and notation is accompanied by terms such as 'understand' and 'perform' (see Endnote 1), rather than encouraging activities that facilitate children's freedom of expression. In geography, learners should be able to demonstrate knowledge of place and location, and learning outcomes include their being able to describe and understand key geographical concepts (200). All must be assessed with evidence of ambitious targets, pupil attainment and progress ready to hand (8).

With the pressure to perform and demonstrate accountability, it seems that the self-fulfilment of learners is a lesser priority, giving rise to fears about the negative impact this might have on their well-being. Adams, Monahan and Wills suggest that such a means-to-end approach to education focuses the mind 'only in its narrowest sense' (citing Miller 2010, in Adams, Monahan and Wills 2015: 200). This approach might be identified as a hallmark of what the authors refer to as the 'performativity discourse' in which 'teaching to the test can become the main objective' (200). This discourse, or culture, reduces the opportunities for children to learn in a cross-curricular manner, and as Adams et al. point out, due to the increase in requirements to demonstrate progression in learning, holistic approaches to learning are being minimised (199).

Ironically, the National Curriculum also states:

> The national curriculum is just one element in the education of every child. There is time and space in the school day and in each week, term and year to range beyond the national curriculum specifications. The national curriculum provides an outline of core knowledge around which teachers can develop exciting and stimulating lessons to promote the development of pupils' knowledge, understanding and skills as part of the wider school curriculum.
>
> (see Endnote 1)

Yet based on my own experience of working in a school, when one considers the significance placed on fulfilling the requirements of this curriculum, including delivering its full content and preparing children for tests, there actually is little time and space for the elements that 'range beyond the national curriculum specifications.' It is the conjecture of this book however that an extra dimension of learning might be accessed through the curriculum, but when a nuanced perspective on learning is applied. This then does not require more time or space – just a more open mind.

I posit here that the emphasis on progress and results potentially undermines the value of the curriculum areas (such as sport, music and art) that engender success for the more kinaesthetic learner, and places an unfair priority on the cognitive dimension of schooling. Means-to-end teaching also affects authenticity, with children being led to meet pre-determined outcomes rather than self-directing their learning. As such, the opportunities for the existential aspects of identity and meaning-making that are essential to inspiring a developing sense of self are reduced, which in turn raises concerns for the mental health of both teachers and learners.

Within the performativity discourse, and in addition to curriculum demands, it must be highlighted that the inspection framework for primary schools also raises concerns. In England and Wales, the inspection body is referred to as Ofsted (Office for Standard in Education), and since 1992, Ofsted inspectors have visited schools to examine practice and policies. Each visit evaluates a school's effectiveness according to criteria set out in each framework document, with different frameworks (historically) having had different foci, ranging from assessing inclusion (2006), to evaluating school's safeguarding practices (2013). Judgements range from 'outstanding' (2018: 41) at one end of the spectrum, through to 'inadequate' at the other (42). Schools in this latter category 'require special measures' (34) and become subsequently subject to external interventions and regular reviews in order to assure that they meet the required standards for success (35).

It is fair to say that the goalposts have changed somewhat over the past 25 years that the inspection body has been at large, with guidelines and criteria evolving and being adjusted in response to public opinion and sociocultural influences. For example, with inspection guidelines having previously placed a high priority on planning and marking, the 2018 inspection handbook emphasises that lesson plans, evidence of marking and the grading of lesson observations are not required. Photographs of children's learning experiences and annotated verbal responses, the acquisition of which until recently seemed to dominate the contact time of teaching assistants, are similarly not to be sought out (2018: 13–16). This might be considered a good thing. Nonetheless, an emphasis on the professional practice and development of teachers no longer seems to be a priority; therefore, the progress from good to outstanding teaching is not so prominent, and classroom practice is not evaluated to the same extent as it was in previous years (for example, in 2015). One might then consider the role of both the teacher and the learning environment to be devalued, whilst the acquisition of data and evidence of progress takes centre stage.

It is worth acknowledging as intimated here that since some of the more demanding elements of accountability have now been minimised, energies potentially can be better applied to creating quality teaching experiences. Yet, as the evidence required for inspections includes published performance data, in-year results and progress monitoring (NEU 2018: 14–15), it might be argued that what happens existentially in classrooms becomes secondary to the requirement to meet the demands placed on schools from external bodies. The priority then is placed on delivering the educational areas or subjects that can quantify success.

In addition, the publication of results and subsequent placing of schools on league tables emphasises the shift described above. In the 'performativity discourse,' what is deemed significant in school life is that which is measurable. As a result, the quality teaching and learning experiences that many teachers enjoy, but which cannot be monitored, become devalued. Arts-based subjects provide pertinent examples of this. This scenario is summed up in the protests of a group of parents in Southern England, who were concerned that due to shifts in Government priorities, the 'curiosity, confidence building …. and embracing creativity' that they valued in their local schools would 'be forced to change' (NEU 2018: 10). In the light of such a scenario, Layla Moran MP, referring to schools as 'exam factories,' has suggested that inspections and the testing of 11-year-old children should be abandoned (9). Layla Moran is a member of Parliament for the Liberal Democrat Party in England.

Noted by a national teaching union as 'harmful,' the emphasis on data and results in England has changed the dynamic of the classroom. A blog post from a teaching-focused online publication (September 2018) argues that inspection reports and gradings, as well as local and national league tables, have incited negative competition between schools, which in turn has de-skilled teachers and disempowered school leaders.[3] Such rhetoric is underlined in the observations made by Professor David Hopkins at the British Education Studies Association (BESA) conference held in 2018. Here, he outlined that the 'wrong drivers' are now being applied to educational experience within the primary school. Instead of valuing group dynamics and identity, the current paradigm prioritises individual success. Instead of developing children's capacity for learning, teaching now requires stricter accountability, and instead of considering, debating and exploring pedagogy, teachers are now limited by what can be presented or measured by technology (Hopkins 2018). The points raised here, as will be outlined in due course, reflect a global as well as an English concern.

In an article published in 2017, researcher Amanda Keddie, who undertook studies in five English primary schools, evaluates the impact on headteachers and teachers of 'external accountability demands.' Citing standardisation, targets, judgements and comparisons as examples, she expresses a worry that what counts as success in schools is externally driven. She also raises concerns that education is equated with productivity and this she argues, incites 'ontological insecurity' (2017: 1246). This maxim, drawn from the writing of Stephen Ball (2003: 220), highlights that the 'creativity, autonomy and intellectuality' of teachers are undermined as their professional existence serves to meet government demands (Keddie 2017: 1246). The various responses of the school leaders involved in Keddie's research illustrate this insecurity, which is often accompanied by fear, inauthenticity and an 'underlying sense of anxiety' (1245). For example, in the article, all participants indicate that judgements on what is valuable or effective in education is now controlled by the inspection body (1250), and that in the move away from teaching creatively, practitioners become limited in their own abilities to be creative or critical, instead, complying to the prescribed regime (1251).

It is important to note that neither Hopkins, Keddie or myself suggest that achievement is not important. I do advocate that it is vital that standards remain constant and upheld; therefore, having a National Curriculum and inspection body ensure that all children have the same access to a good quality educational provision. Indeed, in Keddie's research it is indicated that the school leaders welcomed external accountability as a significant element of what enabled them to keep on track and make progress. What they objected to, akin to Hopkins' assertion, was that as the imposed external drivers are not necessarily educationally value-laden, but laden with performative criteria, they bear no relation to the individuals, the community or the range of experiences that are at the heart of a primary school. Keddie states: 'for these teachers, measures such as Ofsted distort the reality of their school in not accurately capturing what the school is about' (2017: 1251). As such, any 'authentic' learning experiences, or those that might pertain to the existential, communal or even spiritual dimension of education remain at the fringes of school life.

As the National Education Union in the UK notes, the focus on data and results is 'taking the joy out of teaching and learning' (NEU 2018).[4] At time of writing, an announcement made by the Chief Inspector for Education in England, Amanda Spielman, indicates that from September 2019, a more balanced method of judging schools in inspections will be adopted. She writes:

> The proposed 'quality of education' judgement therefore brings together the essential ingredients of education: the curriculum; the teaching, and the assessment that provides the feedback loop; and the resulting outcomes. This judgement is intended to restore

curriculum – largely 'missing in action' from inspection for more than a decade – to its proper place, as an important component of the quality of education.

(Ofsted 2019)

It remains to be seen what this will look like in practice and it will become evident in due course what extra demands it might place on school leaders, subject leaders and classroom teachers. Nevertheless, the concern of this book is not to critique the National Curriculum or inspection body specifically, but to highlight how practitioners might address the issues that arise as a result of the performativity culture in schools. One way of rethinking these issues is by considering the learning that takes place 'beyond the objective.' I am pleased to point out that this approach does not require anything more of teachers or staff in primary schools; it just requires a change in perspective.

As the continuing discussion will reveal, recognising the learning that goes beyond the objective allows teachers and learners to explore the space between the given external structure of education and the actions, reflections and meanings of children. This space might be quite uneven; it might incite taking a risk, possibly to the point of re-thinking who the teacher might be. But it is also proposed that as individual and collaborative agents, children might respond to their learning in a way that is authentic to them. As a result, they might experience transformation and in turn inspire local and global change.

It is suggested here that the performative culture in England is mostly pertinent to the school experience of children in Key Stage One (age 5–7 years) and Key Stage Two (7–11 years). Interestingly, the curriculum for children in the Early Years Foundation Stage (EYFS) is much more holistic, directed towards the individuality of the learner, with open-ended learning, creativity and play forming key features of pedagogy. This is illustrated in the requirements for Early Years education which include assertions such as 'practitioners must consider the individual needs, interests, and stage of development of each child' (Department for Education 2014: 9), let 'children investigate and experience things – and have a go' (10), as well as 'learning and development must be implemented through planned, purposeful play and through a mix of adult-led and child-initiated activity' (9).

Critical educators would suggest that the EYFS framework is not entirely child-centred due to the rigorous expectations placed on teachers to monitor and evidence children's progress (Department for Education 2014: 13). Practitioners also need to scaffold children's educational experiences according to the set early learning goals which include *communication and language, physical development, mathematics* and *understanding the world* (7–8). Nevertheless, it must be acknowledged that children in Early Years settings are certainly provided with a range of opportunities for self-development and self-directed learning. The four principles of EYFS, *The Unique Child, Positive Relationships, Enabling Environments and Learning and Developing* (6), each value child participation with respect for self and others. Furthermore, active learning such as play and exploration, creativity and critical thinking are much more of a priority here than in the later years of school.

Whilst being both encouraging and hopeful of a less performative learning culture, the final months of the EYFS, however, involve children transitioning to more formal learning situations which then become fully implemented at Key Stage One. The difference between the two stages of schooling are remarkably stark. Not only are classrooms arranged more formally with tables set out for stationary rather than open-ended learning, parents are kept at more of a distance from the classroom setting, and a timetable with discrete subject areas is more in evidence. Homework begins in Year One (age 6), and by the end of Year Two (age 7) children are expected to undertake tests which formatively assess their achievements in the Key Stage. The transition from child-directed learning to formative teaching and assessment is swift; yet not all children develop at the same rate and so I am sure that many children in this period are expected to engage in learning experiences that they are not yet ready for. Rory McDowall Clark describes the transition as such:

> Children commonly enter Reception (class) up to a year before statutory school age so are entitled to the play-based, open-ended learning opportunities of the EYFS; in practice, downward pressure from Key Stage One means that choices are restricted and activities are designed to meet formal learning outcomes with emphasis on literacy and numeracy.
>
> (2016: 43)

McDowall Clark also points out that in Britain (including Ireland), children start formal schooling at a younger age than that of many European neighbours. In Bulgaria, Finland and Serbia, for example, formal schooling starts at age 7, which is precisely the age at which they are tested in Britain. McDowall Clark issues a warning here, arguing that children who begin formal schooling before they are developmentally ready can 'lose motivation and become disaffected' (2016: 44). Focusing on what children 'know' and what they 'can do' creates a culture in which there are successes and failures, even at such a young age. This has the potential to affect certain children's view of themselves as learners in a less than positive way. He writes: 'this indicates the disparity between schools and Early Years philosophy and highlights the importance of sensitive transition practices to ensure the continuity of experience for children' (44).

In many ways his more ideal notion of the continuity of experience is reflected in the educational principles of the schools established by Rudolph Steiner. Reference to Steiner education is made in the final chapter of this book; however, there is some value here in recognising the importance of Steiner's view that 'we do not educate children only for childhood, but for their whole earthly existence' (1968/1997: 11).[5] Steiner's practice of grouping children developmentally, not chronologically, and of providing developmentally appropriate activities (such as physical and imaginative learning in the years up to age 7), as well as emphasising the social and democratic aspect of schooling, redresses the concerns raised here and becomes an antidote to the individualistic nature of the performative culture which exists at this time.

In conclusion to this overview of the nature of primary schools in England, including the significance of the learning objective as an assessment tool, it might be fair to say that while the agenda for Early Years education reflects an encouraging understanding of the value of the learner's existence (including interests, feelings and personality), the overall aim of education in England seems to be for achievement, progress and academic success. These values are somewhat antithetical to the existential values that I suggest educators should acknowledge, and rather cynically I suggest that since creativity, imagination and the personal aspects of learning have less economic value, they in turn have less value in the overall perceived success of a school. As already indicated, this situation is not only in evidence in England (and the wider UK), but seems to be prevalent more globally. Therefore, the next part of this chapter makes a brief visit to other educational arenas and highlights similar concerns.

A global concern

As Adams, Monahan and Wills point out, issues regarding a means-to-end paradigm are in evidence much wider than an English context (2015: 199). Similar problems are highlighted by Australian researchers Polesel, Dulfer and Turnball. In their report of 2012 they note the negative impact of high stakes testing and the publication of results on children in state primary and secondary schools in their own milieu.

Noting that class time was becoming dominated by preparations for testing, the researchers observed that such educational experiences promoted self-doubt amongst learners (2012: 9), raising concerns in terms of mental health and self-esteem (8). They noted that teaching to the test involved practitioners excluding wider areas of the curriculum; subjects not tested were 'reduced in importance relative to subjects that are' (9).

As well as having an impact on the culture and environment of a school, Polesel et al. suggest that the performativity culture is responsible for both teacher and student stress. Their research findings indicate that 75 per cent of teachers felt that external pressures induced behaviours such as crying, sleeplessness and sickness amongst students (2012: 18–21) whilst the teachers themselves felt that their integrity was being compromised (10). In response to this report, Adams et al. note that within this performativity culture, the 'whole child' is becoming lost (2015: 199). Test results and the reputation of the school through league tables become instead the dominant foci. The authors suggest that redressing the balance, as well as adopting a different approach to the curriculum, would result in better mental and physical health for learners (200); yet this currently seems an impossible task. However, it is suggested here that in adopting a perspective that recognises learning beyond the curriculum, practitioners might come some way to once again valuing the whole child, including acknowledging who they might 'be' in their existence. The idea of existence will be explored in Chapter 2.

In 2015, Ian Hardy published a philosophical reflection on the rise of such performative measures in the Australian education system. Locating his research in a Queensland primary school, he relates his observations to concerns about educational practice and its value, resonating with what has already been described. For example, Hardy's survey of educational accountability includes the prominence of tests, 'trust in numbers' and the quantification of educational experiences. He argues that such one-dimensional factors now equate to 'what constitutes education' and that the more complex, multiple and life-enhancing purposes of education are marginalised (2015: 468).

Critiquing this paradigm, Hardy asserts that the priority of accountability dictated the culture of the school he studied. This dominant force influenced the practice of teachers who adopted closed-ended teaching methods and subsequently implemented interventions for those learners who were slow to make progress (2015: 476). From a philosophical perspective, this culture shaped what was considered as educational capital. School practices were tailored to meet the requirements of data production and analysis, whilst children's work in books and on displays were 'construed as useful vehicles for monitoring student's performance' (479). Hardy furthermore observed that students themselves now 'spoke the language of assessment and data' (479). As indicated earlier, the form of pedagogy in this culture is reductive and uncritical, resulting in an educational structure that does not consider any inherently personal work to be as meaningful as that which can be assessed.

This structure is also in evidence in the *No Child Left Behind* Act of 2004 (NCLB),[6] and the more recent *Every Student Succeeds Act* of 2015 (ESSA),[7] both promoted across the USA. The rhetoric of the former, signed by President George W. Bush, is reminiscent of the examples already presented here. Terms such as standards, progress, data and improvement all feature on the first page of the programme outline, whilst the second page also contains familiar vocabulary such as assessment and standards. It has of course been debated in America as to whether this programme actually *did* leave children behind.

An article by Helen Ladd (2017) argues that NCLB is a deeply flawed federal policy. The programme, which secured test data and progress on all the students selected for a sample (2017: 463), including those from disadvantaged or marginalised subgroups (464), has also 'shown it has narrowed the curriculum by shifting instruction time toward tested subjects and away from others' (464). Ladd continues: 'This narrowing of the curriculum undermines the potential for schools to promote other valued capacities, such as those for democratic competence or personal fulfilment' (464–465). Regarding the programme's successor, signed in 2015 by President Barak Obama, it is noted that ESSA does not necessarily improve on NCLB, as it neglects to de-emphasise the significance of test results, and further to their value in terms of accountability, these scores are used in assessing teacher ability and inviting intervention in the schools that struggle to meet the standards set in the Common Core State Standards (Washington Post 7/12/15).[8] In claiming to provide access to high-quality education for all children, both programmes seem to limit children's learning experiences, again placing significance only on the curriculum areas to be assessed.

From the perspective of Japan, Dorothea Filus notes that her country is often praised for its excellent academic outcomes, especially in mathematics, science and reading. Yet, as many critics (even from within Japan) note, a pedagogy which emphasises rote learning over creativity and criticality is inadequate for preparing students to participate in an increasingly global and multicultural society. Outcomes-based educational methods have been blamed for social problems such as bullying and violence. Research also indicates that the pressures placed on students to conform often result in seclusion and sometimes suicide (2018: 135). Filus writes: 'education became synonymous with rote learning, thereby suppressing students' independent critical thinking and the development of their own individuality' (137). She furthermore notes that in response to this educational crisis, a new approach to learning referred to as 'relaxed education' was introduced in the early years of this century. Providing learners with more opportunities to assert agency, with the teacher adopting a less dogmatic approach, it seemed that there might be hope of different outcomes. However, she argues that this scheme was ineffective. It transpired that the new methodology was not fully understood and further changes were required (137–138). From a philosophical point of view, the relation of self and other, which is pertinent to redressing the balance between the two extremes described here will be explored in the following chapters.

Writing from a Scandinavian context, Brooks Hall and Sivesind consider the influence of the country's inspection policies on education. Identifying these as a dominant cultural force, the authors observe how the inherent focus on data and testing creates systems which enforce a top-down approach; such systems consciously influence the 'actions of those involved' (2015: 430). Again, practitioners within this education system are at the mercy of those who define norms and promote regulation. Brooks Hall and Sivesind describe how in Norway, schools are inspected annually and note how educational policy emphasises performance-focused accountability mechanisms such as national testing (2015: 437). In Sweden, regular inspections require evidence of a systematic improvement in competency, exchange of knowledge and experience. As much as the latter scenario is more educationally value-laden, the authors point out that knowledge building is measured in performative and pragmatic terms, thus equally driven by external motivators (442).

As well as citing examples from the UK, Australia, USA, Japan and Europe, it would be possible to provide case studies pertaining to the 'performativity discourse' in a plethora of educational situations, each indicating some level of hegemony on the part of those who drive the expectations for success. It would also be possible to describe in general terms the loss of individuality, criticality and creativity of the teacher. As Singh indicates, across the globe, 'learning and quality teaching are increasingly aligned to the discourses of neo-liberalism or the ideologies of the market' (2015: 364), meaning that learners have become commodities or consumers and schools have become regulatory bodies that must succumb to a globalised discourse of learning (366).

In the rhetoric of nineteenth-century German philosopher Hegel, one might describe the performativity culture described here as an example of mastery. In the relation between the learner and the demands of the education system, the latter has more power, authority and subsequently control. In Hegel's illustration, a bondsman (slave) in relation to his master is subservient to him. Yet it is also recognised how the slave performs his 'work' in the image of the master, resulting in the slave becoming identical with the dominating presence of the master (Hegel 1977: 123). Thus, when teachers and learners are required to become subservient to the means-to-end requirements issued by Governments and other educational bodies, they become, like the slave, identical not only with other learners across the nation, but identical with what these external 'drivers' expect them to be. The result is that education becomes inauthentic to the Being of teachers and learners, and moreover, as Hegel might suggest, highlights the illusion of 'success.'

This notion of illusion is reinforced through Hegel's master and slave relationship which serves to illuminate the problems that arise when consciousness aspires to its own independence (Hegel 1977: 113). As much as means-to-end education aims for equality of provision for all, in fact, this is an illusion of equality, since in standardising children's educational experiences, what makes them successful learners – that is, their identity has been reduced, potentially devaluing and demotivating participants in schools.

However, it is possible that some educational ideas might turn mastery on its head. When the existence of the individuals, be they the teachers or learners, is placed in the centre of the learning experience, different outcomes might be achieved. As the discussion unfolds, it will become clear how the primary school classroom in any global context might be and remain a safe space in which children can learn in the light of their existence as well as engage critically with the world.

Educare

According to David Tacey, the concept of education comes from the Latin word *educare*, which means 'to lead out' (2004: 59). In a sense, it leads out what is already within. It concerns leading learning away from externally placed constraints, so to transcend educational norms. The essence of *educare* has a strong resonance with the ideas of some historical educational pioneers. The ideas of early Years educators such as Rousseau and Froebel, as well as the twentieth-century educational philosophers Dewey and Freire are still influential today and their thinking provides a welcome deviation from the problems of performativity. A brief glance at their philosophies highlights how learning need not always to be means-to-end, and will introduce concepts that will be explored further in due course.

Born in Switzerland in 1712, Jean-Jacques Rousseau's view on both childhood and education continue to frame the development of modern democratic concepts such as equality and liberty. His book *Emile* (1762/2016) tells the story of a young boy, representing childhood, who is educated in the countryside by a tutor, representing education. As the child here is perceived as 'innocent rather than simply ignorant (2016: 18),' the role of education then is to let him develop according to his own interests and values. This insinuates that education involves forming persons who 'learned what they needed to know' (18). In Book Two of *Emile*, Rousseau illustrates this by explaining that each child is an individual with his or her mind having its 'own form.' Thus, he exhorts his reader to allow each child's character to reveal itself, to see the learner 'as he really is' (34).[9] Rousseau also indicates how knowledge acquisition, including facts about dates, kings and geography, is not necessarily the foremost principle in education. He suggests that engagement with any natural learning context might be just as valuable. Regarding Emile: 'his whole environment is the book from which he unconsciously enriches his memory' (44).

The notion of child-led learning is also promoted in *Emile*. Rousseau indicates that children must be the drivers in their learning journeys so that they might find their 'proper place in the world' (Pound 2011: 51). Likening discovery-learning to a kind of experimental physics, his suggestion here is that any first port-of-call in education should involve 'sense-experience' which should not be eschewed in favour of books and reason. His argument is that learners should develop their own reason based on their sense-experiences rather than adopting the reasons of others (51).

On taking a closer look at the four principles for the EYFS framework in England, there are remarkable similarities with the ideas of Rousseau briefly outlined here. For example, the first idea of recognising children as individual learners is reminiscent of 'The Unique Child.' The second point, in favour of the context as a learning tool reflects 'Enabling environments.' Finally, the idea of sensory experience leading learning resonates with the active and creative learning within the principle 'Learning and developing.' Therefore, in terms of considering learning 'beyond the objective,' both in Early Childhood and in the continuing years of primary school, Rousseau's ideas have a part to play.

Friedrich Froebel was a German pioneer active during the Romantic period in the early nineteenth century. He introduced the idea of the 'kindergarten' which is often considered the relative of contemporary Early Years settings including Nurseries and Infant Schools. Froebel's meaning of 'kindergarten' is twofold. Translated as 'children's garden,' it refers to the emphasis placed on outdoor education, including the planting, nurturing and harvesting of vegetables and the like, as well as caring for animals (Pound 2011: 13). On the other hand, the kindergarten is an environment in which children themselves might develop and grow, and much like flowers, unfold their potential to be transformed from within.

Again, not unlike the framework for Early Years education, Froebel's philosophy has three main foci: the unity of creation, respect for children as individuals and the importance of play. The child is encouraged to express him or herself freely, able to develop at his or her own pace. At the same time, it is the role of the teacher to empower each student, guiding them through activities and allowing them to make connections between learning experiences (Manning 2005: 372). Play is the means by which children are able to construct meaning (373), and his songs, dances and 'gifts' are the tools with which children might develop intellectually, socially and spiritually (McDowall Clark 2016: 32). In respect of Early Childhood then, the notions of freedom and self-expression prioritised by Froebel and Rousseau do inspire the 'leading out' or even 'learning beyond' as described above. I suggest therefore that when considering an existential perspective in teaching and learning, the ideas presented here might be given some attention.

On a wider educational platform, John Dewey, active in America in the late nineteenth and early twentieth centuries, believed education to be the interaction of learners with their environment, that is, experiential. As such, his approach considers that external factors should be minimised in favour of the child's spontaneous interests. He advocates using resources that kindle children's imaginations, curiosity and skills (McDowall Clark 2016: 34). However, making meaning and interpretation in the light of experience are key aspects of his philosophy that take us further than the pioneers introduced just now. Dewey does not concern meaning in the sense of facts or head-knowledge. Meaning, or 'knowing' is more akin to a resonance than the actualisation of concepts and ideas.

As his text *Experience and Nature* (1938/2008) reflects, the existential qualities of intuition, sense, feelings and perception that contribute to learning exist in a dimension other than the cognitive (2008: 235). Thus, whereas the mind involves 'a whole system of meanings' (229), experiential learning is concerned more with *awareness* or the *perception* of meanings. These meanings are for the here and now; they might be intermittent, vague and not specifically actualised in language (230). However sometimes, the meaning of such awareness and perception unfolds 'like a series of signal flashes or clicks' (233), and following a continuum of meaning making, leads the individual to contribute to the transformation of agreed meanings and attitudes (233; 239). Thus, learning is holistic, integrating sense, emotion and will; such personalised meanings are also likely to challenge agreed meanings, and this introduces criticality to learning. Dewey even acknowledges that such education might involve tension and pain. This is a Kierkegaardian idea and will be explored in more detail in Chapter 3.

Dewey's notion of experience is also explored in his text *Art as Experience* (1934). In a similar vein to his view of meaning, 'experience' here is again holistic. He aims to avoid the individualising and self-sufficient rhetoric of 'an' experience, focusing rather on how authentic learning might become manifest through the connection of a variety of events, in a movement of flow between individuals and environments (1934: 35). This includes engagement with materials and processes, but also involves the unfolding of ideas. It then prioritises the progression of the learning experience, from the aesthetic moment through to the integration of meaning – not any end result.

This again provides a familiar resonance with the essence of *educare*. Dewey writes about learning as the: 'movement of anticipation and cumulation, one that finally comes to completion and has a satisfying emotional quality because it possesses internal integration and fulfilment reached through ordered and organised movement' (1934: 38). In a journal article published in 2011, Hinchcliffe draws on Dewey's ideas of experience to critique the 'teacher-driven' methods promoted by the UK government-issued document *Pedagogy and Practice* (2004). Hinchcliffe describes the objective fuelled lessons outlined in this document as 'controlled.' Neglecting student voice, 'creative deviancy,' exploration or space, 'from the start, the teacher has an agenda to drive through – and everyone must play their part' (Hinchcliffe 2011: 420). This is very much in contrast to Dewey's integration of the sensory and social in learning, and rather reminiscent of what Paulo Freire terms the 'banking' concept of education (Freire 1996: 54).

Paulo Freire was a political educator who was active in Brazil in the mid to late twentieth century. He is best known for his book *The Pedagogy of the Oppressed* (1970/1996). His liberal educational principles are located in his own specific context of educational activity: that is, he worked amongst disadvantaged and uneducated peoples in South America, encouraging and enabling them to participate collectively and critically in their own self-development. This was praxis-based activity: reflection on the world and action in order to transform it (1996: 106). Critical reflection thus inspired learners to challenge the dominant structures of society and to bring about change. Being likened to a bottom-up approach, he gave a voice to the 'silent' and sought to deconstruct the educational system that 'was one of the major instruments for the maintenance of this culture of silence' (Shaull 1996: 12).

For Freire, a process-focused approach enables the enlightenment and transformation that as suggested here might inform an existential perspective on teaching and learning. This is illustrated by the priority placed on the existence of the learner. Far from being a 'receptacle' to be filled by teachers (1996: 54), learners are allowed to critique the way they exist in the world, considering the world not as a static entity, but something, which like themselves is in process (64). This pertains to the idea of becoming, recognising self-development as something unfinished and incomplete: subject to change (65). As such, measurable learning objectives are not important. But the education of the existence of the individual is imperative. This offers not only a positive method, but one that whilst not irreligious, is humanistic. Based on solidarity and fellowship, it concerns the transformation of whole communities, not just individuals, and rather than inspiring competition (evidenced today in league tables of test results), it affirms co-operation which in turn promotes unity. Again, process not product is a key principle.

As noted above, Freire contrasts his methods with what he calls the 'banking' concept of education, in which 'the teacher knows everything and the student knows nothing' (1996: 54). In this method, the learner is expected to passively adopt the truths that the teacher conveys. Furthermore, 'the teacher thinks and the students are thought about.' As such: 'the teacher confuses the authority of knowledge with his or her own professional authority which she and he sets in opposition to the freedom of the students' (54). Therefore, the subjectivity of the individual learner is denied and what the teacher claims to be true, must also be deemed as true. This represents a paradigm of permanence, which of course is a top-down method, far from the ideal of *educare*.

Shaull points out in the Foreword to the 1996 edition of *Pedagogy of the Oppressed* that education for Freire was a subversive force. He suggests that the principles of liberation and action are indeed relevant for the contemporary developed world (1996: 11) driven by targets, competition and economics. This suggestion might just as well be applicable to the primary school setting. Whilst praxis-based learning is directed against political structures of oppression, attention to children's voices and views can transform on a smaller scale, such as in the classroom or playground. There is no reason to deny that reflection and action on a small scale might not become something more. For example, reflection and action on bullying can lead to greater co-operation amongst classmates. In time, this might lead to engagement in political activities promoting equality.

When reflected back into the wider community of parents and other carers, this can inspire not just local change but change on a wider scale. This idea is illustrated by Antony Swift in the book *Children for social change*. Here the author describes the activities of liberation undertaken by children and early adolescents in a Brazilian street community. In keeping with the principle of the child as the subject of his/her own development (1997: 150), the young people in partnership with a local priest and other church members were able to effect change by developing arts projects, a girl's group and creating employment opportunities. This change also led the way in establishing the ethos and curriculum of the local school (163–180).

At the end of this first chapter, I posit that the philosophies of the educators met here have the potential to be implemented across the primary sector. Later chapters outline how this is possible in practice. For example, the notion of holistic education might be reflected through the Eco Schools initiative[10]; the sensory experience and discovery learning can be drawn from open-ended arts or science activities, and the cultural aspect of the curriculum, which in England includes an understanding of British Values,[11] allows learners to reflect critically on their role in society. 'British Values' is a term used in schools in England and Wales to define behaviours of tolerance and acceptance. The values are: democracy; the rule of law, individual liberty; mutual respect for those with different faiths and beliefs, and for those without any faith.

These practices offer a welcome relief from the negativity associated with the problem of performativity. Each educator in his or her own way considers the existence or Being of the learner to be a priority. Pedagogy involves the unfolding of what is already understood and experienced by learners and as each develops and grows, either through sensory awareness and meaning-making, through engagement with the environment, or through political action, the significance of learning to both the individual and community supersedes the significance of learning objectives or outcomes. In the following chapter, the discussion explores in more detail the philosophy of existence in relation to pedagogy and considers further how this might allow teachers and students to recognise 'learning beyond the objective.'

Notes

1 www.gov.uk/dfe/nationalcurriculum accessed 22 November 2018.
2 See www.theguardian.com accessed 9 May 2017.
3 https://www.tes.com/news/teachers-throw-your-oppression accessed 7 February 2019.
4 https://neu.org.uk/press-releases/ofsted-chief-outlines-changes-education-inspection-framework accessed 7 February 2019.
5 The gender priority marked here is provided in the statement by Steiner and not reflective of the views of the current author.
6 https://files.eric.ed.gov/fulltext/ED483139.pdf accessed 15 February 2019.
7 https://www.ed.gov/essa accessed 15 February 2019.
8 https://www.washingtonpost.com/news/answer-sheet/wp/2015/12/07/the-successor-to-no-child-left-behind-has-it-turns-out-big-problems-of-its-own/?noredirect=on&utm_term=.5fc0cfbb4e43 accessed 15 February 2019.
9 The gender priority marked here is provided in the statement by Rousseau and not reflective of the views of the current author.
10 www.eco-schools.org.uk accessed 14 February 2019.
11 www.doingsmsc.org.uk/british-values/ accessed 11 October 2016.

References

Adams, K., Monahan, J., and Wills, R. (2015), 'Losing the whole child? A national survey of primary education training provision for spiritual, moral, social and cultural development,' in *European Journal of Teacher Education*, 38, No. 2. 199–216.

Ball, S. (2003), 'The teacher's soul and the terrors of performativity,' in *Journal of Educational Policy*, 18, No. 2. 215–228.

Brooks Hall, J., and Sivesind, K. (2015), 'State school inspection policy in Norway and Sweden (2002–2012): a reconfiguration of governing modes?' in *Journal of Education Policy*, 30, No. 3. 429–458.

Department for Education. (2014), *Statutory Framework for the Early Years Foundation Stage*, Cheshire: DfE.

Dewey, J. (1934), *Art as Experience*, New York: Minton, Balch & Company.

Dewey, J. (2008), *Experience and Nature*, Carbondale: Southern Illinois University Press.

Filus, D. (2018), 'Educational reforms in Japan: are they contributing to a sense of wellbeing and happiness among young people?' in de Souza, M., and Halafoff, A. (eds), *Re-enchanting Education and Spiritual Wellbeing*, Abingdon: Routledge.

Freire, P. (1996), *Pedagogy of the Oppressed*, London: Penguin.

Hardy, I. (2015), 'Data, numbers and accountability: the complexity, nature and effects of data use in schools,' in *British Journal of Educational Studies*, 63, No. 4. 467–486.

Hegel, G. (1977), *Phenomenology of Spirit*, Oxford: Oxford University Press.

Hinchcliffe, G. (2011), 'What is a significant educational experience?' in *Journal of Philosophy of Education*, 45, No. 3. 417–431.

Hopkins, D. (2018), Key note address, 'British Education Studies Association' conference, University of Bolton, UK July 2018.

Keddie, A. (2017), 'Primary School leadership in England: performativity and matters of professionalism,' in *British Journal of Sociology of Education*, 38, No. 3. 1245–1257.

Ladd, H. (2017), 'No child left behind: a deeply flawed federal policy,' in *Journal of Policy Analysis and Management*, 36, No. 2. 461–469.

Manning, J. (2005), 'Rediscovering Froebel: a call to re-examine his life & gifts,' in *Early Childhood Education Journal*, 32, No. 6. 371–376.

McDowall Clark, R. (2016), *Childhood in Society for the Early Years*, London: SAGE.

Miller, J. (2010), *Whole Child Education*, Toronto: University of Toronto Press.

National Education Union. (2018), *The Teacher*, St. Albans: Century One Publishing.

Office for Standards in Education, Children's Services and Skills. (2006), *The Special Educational Needs and Disability Review*, Manchester: Ofsted.

Office for Standards in Education, Children's Services and Skills. (2013), *The Framework for School Inspection*, Manchester: Ofsted.

Office for Standards in Education, Children's Services and Skills. (2015), *School Inspection Handbook*, Manchester: Ofsted.

Office for Standards in Education, Children's Services and Skills. (2018), *School Inspection Handbook*, Manchester: Ofsted.

Office for Standards in Education, Children's Services and Skills. (2019), *The Education Inspection Framework* (Draft), Manchester: Ofsted.

Polesel, J., Dulferand, N., and Turnball, M. (2012), *The Experience of Education: The Impacts of High Stakes Testing on School Students and Their Families*, Sydney: The Whitlam Institute.

Pound, L. (2011), *Influencing Early Childhood Education*, Maidenhead: Open University Press.

Rousseau, J. (2016), *Emile*, Wroclaw: Pantianos Classics.

Shaull, R. (1996), 'Forward,' in Freire, P. (1970), *Pedagogy of the Oppressed*, London: Penguin.

Singh, P. (2015), 'Performativity and pedagogising knowledge: globalising educational policy formation, dissemination and enactment,' in *Journal of Education Policy*, 30, No. 3. 363–384.

Steiner, R. (1997), *The Roots of Education*, New York: Anthroposophic Press.

Swift, A. (1997), *Children for Social Change*, Nottingham: Educational Heretics Press.

Tacey, D. (2004), *The Spirituality Revolution: The Emergence of Contemporary Spirituality*, London: Routledge.

2   Being and other

Existence

In Chapter 1, it was illustrated how the culture in primary schools in several countries might be described as performative. Even though the meaning of education reflected in the philosophies of a number of key historical educational figures seems to suggest that learning should involve a 'leading out' of knowledge and meaning, starting with the individual learner within a wider community, this notion seems to be at a tangent to how education is experienced today. It was also acknowledged that the aim of this book is not to encourage teachers to subvert the culture but to help them consider a different perspective on teaching and learning, that is, an existential perspective. This perspective has the potential to inspire learning that does not negate set learning outcomes, but goes beyond them. It also prioritises the existence of learners. This is a philosophical idea; hence this chapter is devoted to critically examining what existence means and how this might become a feature of learning in schools.

The current discourse of Philosophy of Education seems to embrace the need for a perspective on education that renegotiates performativity. This is illustrated by assertions made in the *Journal of Philosophy of Education*, published in 2017. For example, Icelandic scholar Atli Hardarson claims that educational policy which 'emphasises competition and economic efficiency' lacks purpose. He argues that analogous to bridges to be built or ports to be steered to, the primary motivator in learning, or what is deemed valuable, is what is to be achieved. Yet as he suggests, 'if we focus exclusively on the external effects of instruction, we miss the vital elements of education that enable people to flourish through teaching and learning' (2017: 62–64). This raises the question:

> how might we recognise these vital elements and embed them within the present culture of school and learning?

Similarly, US-based educator Tyson Lewis argues that as a per-formativity culture has reduced education to 'mere socialisation' into a pre-determined order of things, a differentiated view of what ed-ucation means that expands beyond such limitations is required. In an attempt to encourage an educational perspective that is directed away from socio-economic or capitalist drivers, his use of the word 'beyond' suggests that learning (to meet external criteria) is only one aspect of what education might entail (2017: 230–231). This raises an-other question:

> how might we recognise the learning that takes place beyond set requirements, and nurture them for the sake of the well-being of all?

These questions set the stage for a further exploration of what the 'beyond' might mean. Therefore, in the current chapter some players are placed on the stage. These players are philosophers. Through a critical engagement with their ideas, applying them to contemporary situations and highlighting further issues to explore, I suggest we might become clearer as to how we recognise and teach for that which is 'be-yond' performativity. In an existential perspective of education, the learner rather than the end result of learning is the priority. Thus, the *a priori* elements of existence and Being – which exist way before the es-tablishing of curricula, aims and objectives – are key themes here. The philosophy of Martin Heidegger is a good place to start.

It is important to note that Heideggerian thought is not without cri-tique in my work and cautions will be applied in due course. Neverthe-less, when we consider learning to be less about end results than the existence of the learner that learns, starting with an Heideggerian per-spective is a valid proposition. In Heideggerian philosophy, Being is considered as the genesis of learning; not only is education concerned with meaning, it is also concerned with the meaning of the Being of the learner who exists. 'Meaning' here does not equate to cognitive mean-ing, as in the meaning of phrases or ideas; it does not entirely equate to the kind of affective meaning proposed by Dewey. It is rather to do with the undefined potential of a person or entity, which is *a priori* ahead of any definition or representation. Thus, in an Heideggerian framework, within Being is the potential for unlimited and undirected meaning making, in the world and alongside others.

Heidegger's most influential work is the substantial text *Being and Time*, which developed behind the scenes over a number of years through lectures and seminars and was produced almost 'on de-mand' in 1927 (Krell 1978: 16–17). This work includes the proposition

that philosophy requires an inquiry into how human Being is perceived and understood, and stands at a tangent to, for example, the
knowledge-theory paradigm of Descartes and those of his 'school' (9)
who prevalent at the time, were concerned with subjective representation. Although Heidegger claims that in the light of the maxim 'cogito
ergo sum,'[1] Descartes 'is credited with the departure point of modern
philosophical inquiry,' he calls for a new priority for the 'I' that thinks
and argues that it is not until the nature of Being has been determined
that subjectivity can claim authenticity (Heidegger 1962: 72).

According to Heidegger, Being is deemed an essential state which is
'as it is.' The designation given to Being is *Dasein*, which is the *a priori*
condition for existence. It therefore 'is' before the self might be considered as an entity. *Dasein* pertains to potentiality, meaning that there
are no constraints on what it might be or become as self-development
ensues. Since *Dasein* includes Being, with its hallmark 'Being to be'
(1962: 33), each *Dasein* establishes the foundation for an authentic understanding of self which is reflective of one's own essential state and
the possibility that it inspires.

Heidegger is prudent about not pre-describing any meaning or identity to Being. It is only when the meaning of the existence of the learner
is recognised as the potentiality for learning, that the openness of Being might inspire the development of an authentic self that subjectively
learns. Thus, *Dasein* establishes the foundation for an authentic understanding of self. As it is pre-ontological, *Dasein* exists prior to the
Being of the individual; to be truly authentic to Being, there can be no
fixed sense of self, or other. In other words, *before* recognising children
as learners who have the ability to read or write, play an instrument or
do number problems etc., it is important to acknowledge that they first
and foremost exist as individuals with their own meaning, and within
this meaning is the potential for self-development. This then inspires
learning that transcends what is externally determined.

This self-development is revealed through what Heidegger terms
'care.' It might be suggested that care is the projected form of *Dasein*
that reveals who a person is (1962: 241) as per their personal identity
(241). But it is also self-projective and when *Dasein* is described as being 'ahead of itself in care,' the child whose outward identity is presented is not a determinate entity as suggested just now, but a Being
towards his or her own potentiality-for-Being (236). Ahead of itself
in the projection of the Being that is in a continual state of becoming, *Dasein* understands the possibility of its Being as care (Heidegger
1978: 238). The idea of 'becoming' is resonant with that of Freire, as
described in Chapter 1.

Heidegger differentiates between two existential states: existentia which is actuality and essentia which is possibility (1962: 67). Existentia is the name for the realisation of something as it appears. This constitutes knowledge of an object or reality and the acceptance of this as truth. When education consists of the promotion of knowledge as existentia, not founded on *Dasein,* it results in an inauthentic representation of knowledge. This might also be described as 'falling' – from authenticity into inauthenticity – when Being is taken away. In *this* existential kind of Being, *Dasein* constantly surrenders itself to the world and lets the world matter to it in such a way that somehow *Dasein* evades its very self (220). *Dasein* has fallen away from itself as an authentic potentiality-for-Being into the world of things and ideas. As an entity that is fallen, it has lost its possibility and is cut off from its primordial relationship of Being-in-the-world. No longer is it about becoming, but about being 'enlightened about oneself' and 'knowing it all' (222).

This relates to knowledge that is seen, accepted, interpreted and understood in the realm of public discourse. This knowledge has guarantees and securities which are full of 'truth.' It leads to the synthesising of cultures for enlightenment, knowledge and power, and isolation from the potentiality of each (1962: 223). The aim is for 'averageness' where *Dasein* is no longer possibility but conformity; all entities look and behave the same and aspire to the same levels of success (164).

This very much reminds me of the standardisation of educational experience that children encounter in various countries due to set curricula, end of year expectations and national tests. Thus, we might ask:

- Is the means-to-end learning that pushes children towards targets and goals authentic to their Being?
- Does it create learners who are cut off from their Being so do not feel they can risk being creative, critical or think outside of the box? Does it limit the individual concerns of learners as they interact their own *Dasein* with the *Dasein* of others?
- How often would a child's concern over an issue of social justice in the playground or on the news result in mathematics classes being cancelled for the class to reflect critically on their feelings and responses to what has happened?

An existential perspective on learning recognises children's potential over and above end results and places as much priority on the meaning of the Being of the learner as what is indeed learnt. But on the other hand, does adopting an Heideggerian perspective mean that children should direct their own learning without heed to knowledge, targets, teachers or formal learning environments? I would suggest not.

Heidegger's concept 'Being-in-the-world' is helpful in understanding how. Far from denoting a physical reality, the idea of 'world' suggests an acceptance of an openness to others who each with their own *Dasein* or potentiality-for-Being exist in the same time and space. 'Being-in' means to dwell alongside or be familiar with others in the world, each understanding the other ontologically, and each allowing the potentiality of the other to become manifest (1962: 78–79). When we consider Being as a priority, in existence *before* the formulation or promotion of methods and models, and embrace educational environments and structures as other, alongside whom we reside, we can see a way forward for an existential perspective.

In the light of Being-in-the-world, classrooms become the physical world in which the *Dasein* of both learners and the teacher are able to explore their own meanings. The curriculum becomes the world of concepts that, rather than singularly prescribing fixed knowledge and ideas, allows for inquiry into the meaning of such ideas in the light of the openness of self, world and others. The lesson plan provides a world of activities and tasks that allow for the potential for further study and questioning, and the learning objective, whilst still the assessment tool, becomes the catalyst for a meaningful learning experience. This can inspire inquiry and authentic meaning making.

An example from practice might illustrate this. In a Year Four music lesson, children were required to explore how to make and change sounds using a variety of methods using water. They were asked to record the sounds and using Information Communication Technology, import the recordings to a computer programme in order to create a class piece. For one child this was challenging; her fear of water meant that she could not participate fully in the tasks without disruption, resulting in her choosing to spend the lesson sitting underneath a table. As a result, this child did not achieve, but the teacher did not encourage her to achieve. From a formal learning perspective, the lesson would have resulted in an unsatisfactory outcome. Nevertheless, in her time alone the child was able to use a whiteboard to draw and write, to negotiate this fearful aspect of the world and find meaning in it. As Being-in-the-world, she was able to bring her *Dasein* to the situation she was in. The existential nature of the environment, the task and the teacher's attitude enabled her to reflect on the reasons for her fear and come some way to confronting them.

In the light of this, I would like to propose that when the teacher allows the lesson to enable children to embrace reflection within the learning environment or setting, using the learning objective as a platform for personal development, the lesson becomes more than a 'means-to-end' exercise but an opportunity for transformation. This certainly is not easy, given the demands on teachers. Yet when the teacher creates the condition for authentic learning, and children evaluate their place in the world in the light of their own Being, responding to the situations they find themselves in, interesting things can happen. This also has implications for the role of the teacher: when the teacher's own *Dasein* allows for the realisation of the *Dasein* of the students, as illustrated above, change can ensue. Nigel Tubbs argues that the teacher who allows students to learn learning itself (2005: 132) as it unfolds 'its own most power for disclosing the essence of all things' (133) is authentic and in turn inspires learning that is meaningful.

It was suggested above that Heidegger's philosophy is not without critique and here it is important to note that whilst existence, potentiality and the openness of Being provide the platform for meaningful learning experiences in the light of Being-in-the-world, there are also cautions to be applied. For example, in his book *The Philosophy of the Teacher*, Tubbs highlights that whilst claiming that the truth of Being is in questioning meaning, thus negating mastery and allowing formal teachers to withdraw, Heidegger perpetuates mastery by assuming that the knowledge gained in an existential manner is that which should direct the current situation (2005: 135). This means that one master is negated for another, placing Heideggerian thought in the same inauthentic category as the examples of 'falling' outlined earlier.

In the light of this, we might consider that as much as the illustration presented here highlights the value of prioritising existence, in an Heideggerian approach, any formal structure for learning, or designated persons, might be treated with suspicion. In this position, there is no 'other' with whom the learner relates; indeed, when learning becomes influenced by 'other,' it pertains to 'falling' as described above. From my own perspective, and as will become clear as this discussion unfolds, the roles of environment and teacher are significant for learning, but might be re-evaluated in order to inspire 'learning beyond the objective.' Thus, they are not negated or minimised but embraced within the learning process.

In wholly adopting an Heideggerian perspective, educators should be wary of any representation that is presented as a totality. In other words, they should withhold from teaching as transmission, refrain

from explicit interventions and likewise direct learners away from accepting the presented facts and concepts that form national curricula.
Whilst the continuing premise of the current discussion highlights
the need for an existential perspective in relation to these educational
methods and structures, at this point I think it is fair to say that whilst
the case study described above highlights the beauty and inclusivity of
Being-in-the-world, the teacher allowing this to happen on a regular
basis would be subject to scrutiny more often than not.

Referring back the Hegelian notion of mastery introduced in
Chapter 1, 'other' which is not 'self,' is the dominant force in setting
the expectations regarding teaching and learning in primary schools.
The 'other' calls the shots, and for existential education, being inauthentic, this is problematic. Yet in the philosophy of Heidegger, it is
the meaning of the individual learner in his or her existence that establishes the truth of the meaning of learning. Thus, learning individuals,
contingent in their Being, must establish the foundation for education, over and above the influence of teachers and teaching assistants
alike. This similarly is mastery (albeit in a different form) and also
problematically inauthentic.

In addition, there is also an ethical dilemma inherent in this position. Whilst Being is intrinsic to the process of coming to 'know'
truth, it must be acknowledged that for Heidegger, Being *is* the truth.
It therefore contains the possibility of allowing for the acceptance of
meanings that might be antithetical to agreed values. Tubbs reminds
his readers that in eschewing the role of thought consciousness in favour of the more authentic *Dasein*, Heidegger placed the meaning of
Being within its own Being and its own time (2005: 135). This perceived
authenticity was allowed to establish itself in opposition to those
deemed to be inauthentic, and this is reported to have had unethical consequences. Historian Hugo Ott reinforces this view, suggesting
that Heidegger's idea that 'the beginning continues to be' validated
the movement of 'inner truth and greatness' brought about by the rise
of National Socialism in the period up to and including World War II
(1993: 22). This illustration reveals the horror of the error of prioritising Being as the question of Being without ethical checks.

The potentiality of *Dasein*, when having chosen authenticity, allows
for creative possibility. However, without an agreed moral code or
framework for right decision-making, one might question by what
criteria something is determined as 'right.' If creative possibility allows for a learner to determine meaning that is, for example, against
British Values,[2] or against common law, implicit within this is the
potential to cause both good and harm. If anything is possible, then

the possible can become anything. Furthermore, it might be argued that potentiality-for-Being, whilst authentic to existence and therefore meaningful to the learner, has the possibility of becoming inauthentic. As soon as the groundlessness of potentiality becomes grounded, that is, the learner accepts the learning as actuality, it then becomes an entity in-itself, with its own form of representation. It thus (using Heideggerian rhetoric) falls into the realm of 'the they' which pertains to all that is standardised and equal (Heidegger 1962: 165). Using the example cited earlier, one might argue then that whilst one child engaged in an existential learning experience under the table in class, if all children were encouraged to confront their fears in the same way, this would lead such learning to fall away from its authentic genesis.

It is important therefore, in considering the notion of 'beyond,' that we think wider than what is learnt either as immediate facts or concepts that can be measured, or wider than a dimension of learning that prioritises the meaning of Being, to one that transcends both. I posit that whilst Heideggerian thought provides an excellent starting point for an exploration of existential education, a more robust understanding of the self in relation to other is required.

'Other' is made manifest in many forms. We might consider the teacher or the school as the other who allows for learning to take place. 'Other' might be represented by the curriculum and learning objectives, which scaffold learning experiences. Wider still, 'other' might pertain to Government legislation, curriculum and inspection frameworks, or even agreed moral values. In this respect, it is necessary to determine how it might be possible to negotiate how the *a priori* nature of Being might be made manifest as possibility, thus allowing the individual learner to be integral to the making of meaning, whilst yet being accountable to the structures within which education is located.

As a side-note, the issue of agreed moral values is also contentious within philosophy of education, and it is not sufficient to generalise in this way. As Judith Suissa points out, any prior moral framework might also be held open to judgement, evoking a sense of confrontation and personal reflection regarding statements of truth (2016: 291). Nevertheless, in the context of the current discussion, the reference to agreed moral values includes those established in law as well as the base-line values (for example, sharing, kindness, listening) promoted within school community life.

It might be suggested that in order to negotiate the self and other relation we might consider the dialogue. The idea of mutuality in dialogue is indeed attractive, in the sense that each are considered as equal partners inspiring acceptance and respect. Nevertheless, a critical view of dialogue notes how each partner might equate to a totality, thus perpetuating the fixed nature of its identity. With nothing between or beyond the relation with which to mediate or negotiate each view, this potentially incites a power struggle which subsequently highlights the illusion of the relation. Another example of the self and other relation is the notion *I and Thou* promoted by German theologian Martin Buber. This notion suggests a mutual relation that recognises an *a priori* presence with which the self is in reciprocal relationship (Buber 1970: 67): with no borders. Each relates to the other ideally, that is, as equals and as the same. It might be suggested, however, that this ontological relation 'in-itself' is also a totality. The unification of self and other equates to an entity which itself is self-identical.

Both views of relation described here are problematised by contemporary scholar Machteld Reynaert who suggests that the proposed freedom of the self in a dialogical approach is misrecognised (2014: 185). According to Reynaert, both the individual and external structures for learning have the same self-sufficient status: the autonomous learner is an entity 'in-itself' in relation to the educational environment that is also an entity in-itself. This relation, as will be outlined further in due course, equates to completion and systematisation as well as to self-certainty (Levinas 2003: 37).

Reynaert also argues that any mutual relationship of self and other can never be fully equal. She describes how in such learning situations, one partner will always have the upper hand (2014: 180). As such, she critiques the image of the teacher as a guide or facilitator, which implies a mutual learning journey in which both teacher and learner make discoveries together as equals. As she observes, power is present implicitly; the guide *does* know the way ahead and will direct the journey accordingly (184). In a sense, the relation in-itself might be also described as means-to-end, with the two-way interaction being its own self-serving unit. There is no 'beyond.' Therefore, what is needed is a new understanding of the relation of self and other which is understood in the light of the dimension that is beyond each and beyond their relation.

In the discussion to follow, this requirement is addressed through the ideas of the philosopher Emmanuel Levinas. Born in Lithuania in 1905, Levinas was a Jewish-French philosopher whose main body of work, in critique of the ideas of Heidegger, for instance, concerned the recognition of ontology and the meaning of Being as totalities: equal to the totalities they sought to negate. Rather than prioritising Being, Levinas promoted the idea of ethics as the means by which self relates to other and he introduced the notion of the transcendent Other, with whom self and other relate 'infinitely.' The work of Levinas has been valuable in contemporary terms in relation to hospitality and the accommodation of the 'other,' be it in promoting inter-faith conversation, or welcoming refugees. As noted in his New York Times obituary, his philosophy significantly enabled a 'search for the meaning of Judaism after Auschwitz.'[3]

In Levinas' most commonly known text *Totality and Infinity,* authentic relation is encouraged (ethically) through the perception of self in the face of other. It is therefore not just about the self; it accepts difference and recognises the significance of both partners. As much as his writing is not for an educational context per se, the author's ideas lead us to suggest that learning which leads out from one's existence best takes place in the light of 'other.' Equally, 'other,' might only have true meaning when embraced in the light of who learners 'are' in their existence.

Take, for example, a Science lesson which requires learners to label the different parts of a flower. Children might learn the different parts by using online or library-based research, or they might remember the information taught to them in class. To make the learning more meaningful, children might be provided with real flowers to observe and dissect. Thus, personal experience (self) prevents the children from participating in a mainly knowledge-based lesson (other). The relation that is established is ethical: it prevents the existential aspect from becoming groundless (or unethical as intimated above) and also prevents the mastery which activates the 'falling' of existence (*Dasein*) to the world of conformity. Each is the checkpoint against which both self and other are evaluated.

Yet it might be argued that this is also a self-serving unit, similar to that described above. In line with Reynaert's argument, even in a dialogical relation, self-reflection is evident (Levinas 2003: 36). This relation might be expressed as A=A (37). This equation is introduced by Chamberlain and Ree who describe the A=A (1998: 28) as self and other, absolute in an absolute relation. It is important to note that Levinas's intention is not to subvert totality; his task is to reimagine self and other in the light of the Other that is beyond relation. This Other is infinity. Thus, Levinas writes about how the self and other relation might be established in relation with Other. The Other is beyond the immediate relation – or beyond both the prescriptive and more open-ended methods of teaching. In the light of his ideas, we might suggest that in order for learning to go beyond the objective, this Other dimension must be in place. I now present a brief overview of his ideas as presented in his key text and highlight how a Levinasian perspective might contribute to our further understanding of learning beyond the objective.

In *Totality and Infinity*, Levinas proposes that his task is to re-imagine the relation of self and other in the light of the Other that is beyond the immediate. The immediate equates to 'totality' (2003: 22–23). This Other is infinity (24). As infinity is beyond representa-tion, it transcends totality and avoids claims to essentiality. As cited above, totality is not negated: however, here the relation of totality and infinity considers the idea of infinity as that which is 'produced in the relationship of same *with* other' (33). Also, as intimated earlier, Being considered as self without the intervention of other, is incited as an example of totality. Nevertheless, infinity recognises the existential self in the relation. Levinas posits that there is 'a gleam of exteriority in the face of other' (24) as each relates to the other face to face.

Infinity is irreducible, therefore has no power over the other and vice versa. Hence, when all ideas are founded on the idea of infinity, any self-sufficiency regarding existence, Being and representation are interrupted (Levinas 2003: 26). Thus, in school, rather than aiming to extrapolate the individual from educational structures, we might con-sider that the individual has the potential to become more fully self-aware in the 'face of the other' rather than just in relation to one's own Being. On the other hand, we might argue that educational structures themselves become more meaningful in the light of the potentiality of the existence of the learner. This warrants further thought.

Historically, Levinas wrote in response to the philosophies of (for instance) Socrates, Hegel and Heidegger, considering their ideas on thought and Being in terms of totality. For Levinas, totality equates to 'the possibility of signification without a context,' and in his text he alludes to objectivity and absolutism (2003: 21), and representation (24) as examples. Additionally, as suggested above, the primal identity of existence is as much identified as totality as that which is absolute (34). This 'I' is self-sufficient, its subjective identity being its own con-tent deemed as truth (36).

In writing *Totality and Infinity,* the author's intention was not to subvert these ideas nor indeed to subvert totality; the task was to reimagine them in the light of the Other that is beyond relation: in-finity. Being metaphysical, Levinas's infinity is a dimension of exter-nality that exceeds 'the knowledge of measuring things' (2003: 34). It surpasses the universality of the 'I' that thinks (21) and cannot be considered as in-itself. Rather, it corresponds to the idea of the Other who is unknowable. Being transcendent, infinity is beyond the representation of 'other,' or facts presented in external and agreed terms. According to Levinas, through representation, the Other would dissolve into the same, thus again resulting in a totality (38). Rather, infinity transcends truth presented as in-itself and avoids any claims to essentiality. Yet equally as immanence, the Other cannot either be reduced to immediate knowledge (27) and so the self-sufficient subjectivity of the learner who is Being is posited as opinion and illusion (23). For authenticity, both teacher and learner must be brought into relation with externality.

The absolutely other that is Other (2003: 39) is 'absolute exteriority' (35) and entirely unknown. Therefore, the relation is imperfect. Levinas is clear that infinity is not an end result to be attained but that which, in an intentional movement, enters the now. This entering is the movement by which the in-itself is ruptured. Learning then is not an evasion of, but an intentional move towards the Other.

On reading this, one might determine that the Other equates to a notion of a transcendent being or power, or absolute Other (signified by many as G(g)od). Yet in respect of ideas presented here, to name or describe the transcendent in such terms is to reduce 'it' to a represented entity (totality) and this is to be avoided. As Levinas asserts, the transcendent is 'other with respect to a term whose essence is to remain at the point of departure, to serve as entry into the relation, to be the same absolutely' (2003: 36). Rather, infinity relates to the dimension of existence that is 'beyond' knowing or reduction yet allows self and other to relate existentially.

This is not easy to grasp, and the reader is allowed to question how this notion is relevant to the primary school classroom. As a first point of call, we might consider Levinas's ideas in summary as the truth of the individual being only evident through dependence on the other (2003: 43) in relation to Other; therefore, in respect of this, we might next consider that the roles of the teacher and learner, and learning, might be re-evaluated in their relation to Other. Finally, we might explore what this could mean in practice and how it might encourage learning that goes beyond the objective.

The role of the teacher here is that of a learning facilitator, who embraces the thoughts and questions of the learners, considering their own life experiences, and helping shape their thinking in the light of the framework provided (the classroom, curriculum, school values, etc.). Relationship is very important and the task of listening is as significant as speaking. The inner life of learners might lead to the creation of meaning, but learning is located within the context of the pedagogical environment. What is significant is how the teacher creates the condition for the learning that allows for the 'beyond' to happen. In respect of Levinas, the most important aspect of learning is that which transcends the immediate learning to face the Other, so to inspire the ethical moment of self-reflection. An example from practice should help to clarify how this might happen in school.

As part of their topic about World War II, class 6 undertook three sessions that focused on the Holocaust, with particular reference to the Auschwitz death camp. Following the National Curriculum guidelines for history, the teacher invited the children to construct knowledge from a range of resources and in groups they wrote an account of what they had learned. They subsequently presented their learning to the class. Following this, the children in pairs devised questions about Auschwitz which they then researched using online media. Finally, they were given the opportunity to write about why they think it is (or not) important to learn about the Holocaust in school, as well as record what they think they should never forget from history. Inspired by the final scene of the film *Schindler's List*, where survivors saved by Oskar Schindler and their actor counterparts placed a stone on his grave, each child in turn read aloud their statement of what they should never forget, and similarly placed a stone on the class altar to form a cairn – a symbol of remembrance (Wills 2018: 250).

During the three lessons, it was evident that the children were able to personally engage with the learning in a way that ensured that their experiences went beyond the fulfilment of the learning objectives. As existential learners, they were able to place themselves in a position whereby they were willing to be moved, shocked and confronted by the learning. The teacher, following the agreed curriculum for history, recognised that certain requirements needed evidencing. Yet she was also aware that a transcendent dimension was present in the classroom, which allowed the children to engage on a deeper and more personal level than was expected (2018: 250–251).

In her book *Mourning becomes the law*, the late philosopher Gillian Rose declared on seeing the film *Schindler's List*: 'it is my own violence that I discover in this film' (1996: 48), suggesting that for her, the film incited more than a recall of events, or even a feeling of sympathy. Her own morality was confronted by what she saw. Similarly, in class, some children themselves were confronted by the learning, one child in particular stating that history teaches us that even minor situations in our own lives can reflect the same (immoral) values. I suggest that this illustrates the Levinasian idea of Other in that the immediate relation of self and other (child and the teacher/history curriculum) is interrupted, or confronted, by a dimension of learning that is deeper than and way beyond what is expected. Using a history lesson as an example, this takes us beyond the notion that there are lessons to be learnt from the past, to an understanding that the curriculum might provide a 'framework within which we can ask pupils to confront human action and moral judgement' (Husbands 1996: 65).

Drawing on ideas from both Heidegger and Levinas, it is possible to recognise that education in the primary school might involve more than a linear progression towards intended results. When the potential for self-development and reflection that is offered by an understanding of *Dasein* is held in balance with an understanding of the importance of the relation of the Being of the learner with the surrounding educational context and culture, and when the teacher provides the condition in which this relation might be confronted or interrupted by an 'Other' dimension of learning, the foundation is laid for an existential pedagogy. This 'Other' is what takes us to the idea of 'beyond.'

In the following chapter, the ideas explored above will be developed further in relation to the educational process *Bildung*, for learning that not only has value for attainment and success but also for the personal life of the individual learner.

Notes

1 Descartes' cogito ergo sum, first used in Latin in his text *Principles of Philosophy* is popularly translated as 'I think therefore I am'. www.journal ofinterest.com/thoughts/cogito-ergo-sum/, accessed 13 June 2016.
2 See Chapter 1, endnote 11.
3 https://www.nytimes.com/1995/12/27/world/emmanuel-levinas-90-french-ethical-philosopher.html accessed 3 January 2019.

References

Buber, M. (1970), *I and Thou*, New York: Charles Scribner's Sons.
Chamberlain, J., and Ree, J. (1998), *Kierkegaard: A Critical Reader*, Oxford: Blackwell.
Hardarson, A. (2017), 'Aims of education: how to resist the temptation of technocratic models,' in *Journal of Philosophy of Education*, 51, No. 1. 59–72.
Heidegger, M. (1962), *Being and Time*, Oxford: Blackwell.
Heidegger, M. (1978), 'Letter on humanism,' in Krell, D. (ed.), *Basic Writings*, London: Routledge.
Husbands, C. (1996), *What is History Teaching? Language, Ideas and Meaning in Learning about the Past*. Buckingham: Open University Press.

Krell, D. (1978), 'General introduction: the question of being,' in Krell, D. (ed.), *Basic Writings*, London: Routledge.

Levinas, E. (2003), *Totality and Infinity*, Pittsburgh: Duquesne University Press.

Lewis, T. (2017), 'Study time: Heidegger and the temporality of education,' in *Journal of Philosophy of Education*, 51, No. 1. 230–247.

Ott, H. (1993), *Martin Heidegger. A Political Life*, London: HarperCollins.

Reynaert, M. (2014), 'Pastoral power in nurturing the spiritual life of the child,' in *International Journal of Children's Spirituality*, 19, No. 3–4. 179–186.

Rose, G. (1996), *Mourning Becomes the Law*, Cambridge: Cambridge University Press.

Suissa, J. (2016), 'Testimony, Holocaust education and making the unthinkable thinkable,' in *Journal of Philosophy of Education*, 50, No. 2. 285–299.

Tubbs, N. (2005), *The Philosophy of the Teacher*, Oxford: Blackwell.

Wills, R. (2018), 'Can learning about the Holocaust be spiritual? Reflections on a teaching and learning experience with Primary School children,' in *International Journal of Children's Spirituality*, 23, No. 3. 248–259.

3   Bildung's Repetition

Self and other

In Chapter 2, it was indicated how understanding the relation of self and other is significant for a new perspective on education. For example, considering the value of the existence of the individual in relation with the wider educational system might allow learning to be more than just a means-to-end transaction (for example, in box-ticking or fulfilling the criteria required for inspections). The ideas of Heidegger (1962) and Levinas (2003) located the discussion in a philosophical framework and these were illustrated by examples from practice that illuminated existential moments of learning.

Nevertheless, cautions were also applied. It was noted how in prioritising the existence of the learner, teachers might potentially incite the same kind of hegemony as they would when external drivers are the primary motivators. Examples of self and other such as the dialogue and Buber's *'I and Thou'* (1970) were recognised as totalities, described here as A=A, and so the need for a more ethical self and other relation was highlighted. Critique was offered through the thinking of Machteld Reynaert (2014).

For Gillian Rose, a contemporary philosopher cited above, the equal relation of self and other is similarly problematic. In *Mourning becomes the Law* (1996), she raises some concerns. First, Rose introduces what she calls mutual recognition. Mutual recognition implicates the self and other relation as a dualism: a self-relation of two forms of consciousness. Each partner is a totality existing 'in-itself' and as self-identical is immediate and ready-to-hand. Consciousness is not self-critical and does not consider what is beyond. In relation with the other which is similarly self-identical, consciousness recognises itself in the other and their relation depends on what is recognised of *themselves* as they relate. In this self-reflection, neither partner would expect to inspire anything new or counter-cultural; it would not consider what is beyond the relation. Rather, in mutual recognition the identity of each is retained and perpetuated.

In practice, this might be illustrated through children and adults co-operating in a School Council arena. Recognition of the merit of listening to students and valuing their opinions has recently inspired schools to create a forum where they are allowed to feed thoughts back from other pupils and make suggestions for school improvement. In dialogue, or mutual recognition, the council members and staff negotiate and discuss possibilities, thinking creatively to take their suggestions forward. In my own context, the School Council have been successful in introducing a wider recycling scheme for local families, whilst participants have also planned and designed activities for younger children to enjoy at play times.

This is all very worthwhile, yet it has Hegelian overtones. Although striving to avoid becoming systematic in allowing the voices of children to be heard, the relation between children and staff (or self and other) in mutual recognition actually is a 'necessary relation' (Lovlie and Standish 2003: 3). This again might be described as A=A. As Rose argues, this is unsatisfactory for authentic learning (1996: 75). As much as the forum allows for change, it only accepts change agreed by staff. Any change is limited to what is acceptable within the system, and as it does not allow for a change *of* system, it falls short of allowing for the potentiality of *Dasein*. As a result, the authentic self of the children is separated and alienated. Rose proposes that for a more authentic approach, educators might prepare for the *failure* of mutual recognition, in what she terms misrecognition. This failure provides the opportunity for the relation to be reworked. In so doing, it is no longer equal.

Allowing for the failure of A=A requires a willingness on the part of each form of consciousness (teacher and student) to revise or redefine their own sense of self-identity as well as the identity they have in terms of the relation. This might be a risky business as at times, the values and opinions of the students might subvert the status quo. In a scenario when teachers are willing to let go of mastery in order to also become learners, this might cause insecurity on the part of the students who are conditioned to accepting their status as recipients of what teachers provide. Nevertheless, when mutual recognition gives way to misrecognition, a different kind of relation emerges.

It is important to note that as misrecognition identifies the relation of A=A as a necessary relation, this does mean that the dual relation of self and other is *not* in-valid. Therefore, the School Council can continue to exist and do good work. Indeed, any examples of adults and children working together in a dialogic situation are worthwhile. But in the light of the assertions of Rose, for an existential approach this is not enough. For true authenticity, the mutual relation must fail – failure being brought about by an interruption. Interrupting opens up the middle space *between* self and other. This is the space which allows for critical reflection and subsequently, I propose, the inspiration of change. This interruption disallows the equality or totality that comes with dialogue, and offers a third dimension, or learning partner, which Hegel, Tubbs and Rose refer to as Spirit (Hegel 1977: 136; Rose 1996: 75; Tubbs 2005: 218).

Again, in my own context, and continuing the theme of recycling drawn from School Council activity, an example of an interruption took place following a choir field trip undertaken with some of the older children in school. During the trip, the children were all very careful not to throw away their crisp packets as the whole school recycling scheme had recently extended to including such items. All were duly kept together and the next day placed in the recycling box in the Junior area. However, during my lesson the following morning, which was about Space, and nothing to do with the previous day's trip, one child became quite agitated. As well as being tired (as we all were), he was also frustrated. Having an additional need, it is usual for him to remove himself from class in times of stress. Yet in this instance, he took himself into the library for a purpose. He needed to deal with what was on his mind: recycling. As the bell went for lunch, he came back to class with a letter written to the organisers of the choir concert, urging them to encourage *all* participants (6,000 children) to recycle their empty crisp packets, as he was aware that in such a context, there would have been a lot of plastic waste.

This interruption (not of the lesson, but of his engagement with the lesson) made us all aware on reflection, that what was significant in that morning's education was not what the children had learnt about Space, or their analysis of the premise of the film *Close Encounters of a Third Kind*; the real (and more meaningful) learning was that inspired by a child who was actually disengaged with the required learning objectives. Indeed, we might go as far as recognising that this child was in fact the teacher. In discussion with this child and the member of staff responsible for eco-education in school, follow-up activities were planned based on this child's intervention, including devising a wider campaign for plastic recycling, writing a blog entry and composing a song – all within yet also beyond the set curriculum, or what might have been discussed at the School Council.

Philosophically speaking, in the failure of mutual recognition inspired by the interruption, each form of consciousness, or in-itself, has truth not only in the relation with other, but in the relation of the relation (Rose 1996: 75). In this example, the self and other relation of teacher (driven by the set learning objective) and students (participants in the lesson), was interrupted by an agitated child, so to take learning beyond the objective and to establish a learning relation with an additional partner. No longer able to describe the relation as necessary or A=A, this subsequently establishes a new shape of learning, described by Rose as triune. In the light of the illustration from school, we might consider how this influences an existential perspective.

The triune shape recognises another 'otherness' which is introduced through the interruption. This 'otherness' relates to the self-relating of the self and other. Not being a part of the totality, or of the necessary relation, this third partner establishes the notion of 'beyond.' Whilst the self and other relation exists as necessary, the third partner transcends the relation, and is able to intervene: mediating and re-evaluating the learning established through immediacy. This 'otherness' or Spirit inspires both the education of the self and the education of the 'self and other' relation. Rose asserts that as each 'self' is constantly being reformed and re-imagined, each learns of itself in a way that is unfixed and unstable (1996: 75). This is one of the hallmarks of an existential perspective: not knowing what the 'end-result' of learning might be. Therefore, there cannot exclusively be fixed outcomes in learning and this throws into question the viability of a purely means-to-end paradigm.

Significantly, and again reminiscent of the critique provided by Reynaert (see Chapter 2), the triune shape ensures that neither self nor other have the upper hand. Student contingency is neither extinguished nor prioritised; the law (or any external influencer) is not the driving factor in existential learning. There is no space for domination or totality (Rose 1996: 75). The interruption of Spirit prevents either the public and private expressions of learning from becoming the dominant aspects of education, and provides the potentiality in the middle space, for education of a different kind. This new kind of education is identified by Rose as 'Bildung.' Rose describes 'Bildung' as 'formation or education which is intrinsic to the phenomenological process' (72). Akin to what has been described here, it is a process of learning that embraces the relational partnership, but also recognises the space between and beyond. As provisional, unfixed and unstable, it is risky; yet it is authentic to both self and other in their relation with the necessary self-relation. Significant to the current discussion, Bildung is explored in some detail now.

Bildung

The educational notion Bildung has experienced something of a renaissance in recent years. In addition to the reference made by Gillian Rose above, the idea has been developed, for example, in the arenas of Children's Spirituality and Philosophy of Education. Bildung concerns the former in relation to the proposition that process-centred education inspires spiritual development. This is illustrated in the writing of spiritual theologian John Pridmore, who describes the spiritual learning process as 'the arousing of awareness already present' (2004: 285). Regarding the latter, the notion of Bildung has featured in recent Philosophy of Education discourse, particularly in Europe, and a 2002 edition of the *Journal of Philosophy of Education* was given over to this theme. Having also been subsequently published as a full text titled *Educating Humanity: Bildung in Postmodernity* (2003), the variety of ideas included in this edition provide a framework for contemporary interpretations of Bildung.

According to Nordenbo, the German word 'Bildung' relates to the noun 'bild' that means image, with the suffix 'ung' concerning process. Thus, it concerns something or someone who actively participates in the process of learning. Here the individual is an agent who in the act of education takes part in his or her own formation or development (2003: 25), the telos of which is individual freedom. Although 'bild' here equates to the learning subject, the idea of the image is also important and will be explored in due course.

Historically however, and in the first instance, it is important that Bildung as proposed by German educator Wilhelm von Humboldt (1767–1835) is given some attention. von Humboldt was a neo-humanist who, anticipating the ontological basis for learning later to be evidenced in Heidegger formulated his own notion of a pre-existing basis of understanding. Whilst this basis was not totally removed from the hermeneutical or linguistic dimension of education, his premise nevertheless encouraged the idea of self-development as the cultivation of being, allowing for the freedom, potential and creativity of individuals.[1]

Presupposing that one ideology, method or model never has the upper hand, von Humboldt's Bildung, which is proposed as the development of the individual within temporality, provided an escape from the hegemonic hierarchies and universalising powers prevalent in his day. As such, he rejected the idea popular at the time that the mind and body were separate in human nature, and in actively seeking to limit the influence of the State, or indeed any other system or structure which prioritised pre-determined ends, he proposed that education should allow for the awareness of being and uncontrolled personal growth. His method has been described as 'upbringing' which concerns the actions of an independent and engaged individual in relation with the learning environment – or in von Humboldt's rhetoric, the world (Nordenbo 2003: 31).

In the early nineteenth century, von Humboldt was involved in reforming schools as well as the early German Universities. These institutions were developed along humanist principles, advocating free and universal education. As noted in the Stanford Encyclopaedia of Philosophy (accessed online 10/01/2019):

> his idea of combining both teaching and research in one institution guided him in establishing the University of Berlin in 1810 (today's Humboldt University) and the structures he created for this institution would become the model not only throughout Germany but also for the modern university in most Western countries.

He is also credited with influencing the thinking of members of the twentieth-century 'Frankfurt School' such as Adorno and Horkheimer. The 'Frankfurt School' is a movement of scholars and thinkers associated, however loosely, with the University of Frankfurt in the early twentieth century. Based on Marxist principles, the members promoted ideas such as critical theory, and sought to reject both capitalism and any super-structures, including religion, that claimed absolute truth.

Regarding Bildung, in his short fragment 'Theory of Bildung' (2000) written in 1793, von Humboldt argues that the purpose of learning is not to gain the contents of knowledge; its purpose is the individual's 'inner improvement' (2000: 58). The learner represents humanity as a 'rich and worthy substance' (59) whose actions do not take place in isolation; rather they occur in relation with 'other' who here is named 'world.' von Humboldt notes that between self and other is 'the most general, most animated and most unrestrained interplay' resulting in the 'attempt of the will to become free and independent in itself' with the possibility of human development (58).

Interplay is a continuous movement in which the individual reaches beyond himself to 'external objects' from the world; following this he reflects back into his own inner being 'that which he undertakes outside himself' (von Humboldt 2000: 59). Of course, it must be noted that the gender priority included here is in line with von Humboldtian rhetoric as opposed to any prioritising on the part of the current author. As it is essential that the individual is not considered as a totality, interplay ensures that there is a 'resemblance' between self and other. The formation of the individual includes engagement with the external environment; on the other hand, the perception of the environment develops as the individual participates in the movement of learning. Thus, Bildung might be described as a process of coming to understanding through the development of the individual's relation with the world.

von Humboldt was concerned that learning as interplay might easily become systematised. This would result in Bildung no longer being a process but 'merely scholarship' (2000: 60). Therefore, he points out that the telos of learning is not what is gained as knowledge. Education is not means-to-end or the fulfilment of prescribed outcomes. Rather it inspires the freedom of the learning individual against the universalising systems and schemes that 'own' knowledge. The systems he refers to might equally concern the religious and political as well as the educational. He writes: 'the ideal becomes greater if one measures the exertion it requires rather than the object that it is to represent' (60); in other words, the action of learning takes priority over the outcome.

In order to evade totality, it is important that in interplay, the relation is also evaluated. Here, self and world are both significant learning partners. They are immediate entities that self-relate. Yet, unlike in mutual recognition, they are linked but not unified. As Lovlie and Standish summarise, 'Bildung starts with the individual embedded in a world that is at the same time that of the differentiated other' (2003: 3). Following the relation, the movement of interplay ensures that each contribute to the learning process; however, the process does not result in the relational partners moving forward together (as in the example of the School Council). There are other dimensions of Bildung that prevent this from happening.

First, von Humboldt's interplay involves a diversity of 'tools,' including the senses and feeling, which allow for different ideas to form regarding an understanding of the world. Senses and feeling, which also might extend to imagination, spirituality and creativity (as per the ideas of Steiner and Dewey explored in Chapter 1), allow for the re-evaluation of what is understood in immediacy. Such aspects of humanity inspire the integration of ideas developed through sensory and emotional engagement and allow learners to develop critical reflection or alternate views regarding what is presented in class. This dimension, which takes learning beyond externally determined outcomes but also transcends the purely personal, provides a platform for creativity, criticality and the formation of new methods or even structures.

The influence of the sensory dimension on immediacy is one means by which the middle space might be opened. Interplay provides a subjective insight, on the basis of the senses and emotion, into the world of learning – which in the primary school is predominantly objective. Thus, through the sensory dimension of Bildung, each individual learner might create his or her own meaning in the light of their engagement with the world. Rather than being 'acquainted with it from all sides' (von Humboldt 2000: 59), or perpetuating a definitive means of learning, interplay contributes to an education that is truthful to students in their existence; it might be argued that this is as truthful as an education of immediate learning driven by curricula, tests and inspections.

Further to the notion of interplay, we might also consider the significance of the process of learning highlighted in Bildung. An example of this is provided by Heins Gunther-Heimbrock in the 1999 *International Journal of Children's Spirituality* (1999: 51–60). Here, Heimbrock describes a study in which children created, evaluated and reformed pictorial representations of God. He observes that having been invited to record their visual impressions, the children began to draw, but over the course of the activity, some rubbed out, started again or reworked their images. As they did so, they allowed their impression of what might otherwise be considered a fixed entity (God) to become a fluid notion, open to evaluation and change. The author proposes that through the process of painting or drawing, interplay had taken place between the children's inner and outer worlds (58). This is an example of creative subjectivity in which the activity influenced not only the end result – that is, the presentation of the images – but also allowed for process-based learning. In this, the learners were given permission to re-imagine any images they might have inherited from a religious culture, the media or from home. Like the image or 'bild,' that is always in process, the representation resulting from interplay is and remains unfixed, always subject to re-interpretation and change (56).

Reflecting on Heimbrock's study, we might note that is the process of evaluation which takes place in the middle space that has educational importance. Whilst acknowledging traditional religious beliefs as a starting point in learning, and not negating but re-negotiating them, Bildung here might be identified as the means by which children become aware of their 'personal capacity to develop their own theology' (Gunther-Heimbrock 1999: 52). For the wider curriculum, it can be deduced from this that as much as an end result is often required (through the meeting of the learning objective), what has meaning for the learner is *how* they come to understand what they learn.

This highlights the value of another dimension of Bildung – children recognising themselves as active learners. We might identify them in this sense as agents of their own learning. Brendan Hyde states that agency is 'the ability of children to understand their world and act upon it' (2010: 93), able to have an influence on education and make meaning for themselves. This is reminiscent of the ideas of Freire (introduced in Chapter 1), who takes this further, indicating how agency involves reflection on the world and action, in order to transform it (1996: 106). As much as Freire's praxis-based learning is directed against political structures of oppression, in the light of the illustration from school presented above, we might accept that a child's agency might not only contribute to transformation a smaller scale as in the classroom, but potentially on a wider scale, to effect systematic change.

In line with agency, the personal reflection dimension of Bildung, which takes place in the middle space between the individual and the world is also significant for learning beyond the objective. In a further example, Bildung as suggested here might be illustrated by the reflections of children aged seven on a series of activities in the curriculum area of physical education.

On a dry Spring day, the children were able to play games outside. On this particular occasion, the object of the lesson was to understand the value of teamwork. Using the playground as a large space for running and playing, the children engaged in such team activities as collecting cones from around the outdoor environment, creating a word using bodies, and playing games such as passing a ball over and through the legs of each player. They also enjoyed using a play parachute to send a ball around in a continuous circle. Each activity ensured that all children not only participated but were necessary to their team's success. As in any team sport, each player had a role. Inclusion of all is vital. Therefore, whilst the children had fun, they also experienced the value of utilising the assets or skills of individuals (for example, fast running, strategic thinking, body strength) for the good of the team.

In the rhetoric of von Humboldt, the lesson within the wider learning context represented the world (other); learners (self) engaged with the world in order to gain a clearer understanding of teamwork through the activities. However, in addition to these valuable lessons, they also gained a deeper understanding of themselves in relation to the learning. When interplay allowed for the creation of a middle space of reflection, an opportunity was provided to take the learning further. Back in the classroom, the children were provided with a paper 'brick.' They were invited in a moment of quiet, to consider what an understanding of teamwork might mean for themselves and the wider school community. They jotted down their ideas on the brick-shaped paper and handed them in at the end of the morning. In this middle space, Bildung allowed for the children's feelings and thoughts to create meaning, so that in some cases their reflections were transformational – for themselves and indeed school life.

> One child explained that the games helped her to understand that all children must be included. She committed herself to looking out for children alone on the playground, in order to befriend or help them in any way.
>
> Another child noted that not all children have the skills required for school life, and decided to help any younger children who might need assistance at playtime in putting on their coats or tying their shoe laces.
>
> Finally, one child related his learning to a wider context, considering how homeless people are excluded in society; his reflections led him to consider how he might help homeless people such as giving food to a food bank.

As much as the time of reflection in this example was instigated by the teacher and not an interruption as in the example presented earlier, it is still clear that in this lesson, the condition was provided for the children to reflect on the creative interplay between self and other that had taken place on the playground. The opportunity was taken for children to think about the value of teamwork *beyond* the objective 'we are learning to work together.' Of course, not every lesson in a primary school is followed by a time of reflection. Nevertheless, the examples offered here indicate how, when space is created, or the middle space between self and other is recognised, learning that is meaningful and transformational can take place.

Over recent years, when leading training sessions pertaining to spiritual education, I have referred to the plenary section of a lesson as the time when children might ruminate on the content of the lesson in order to consolidate learning. The 'plenary' is the part of the lesson when the learning is rounded up. It normally takes place in the final five minutes of the lesson and involves children discussing what they have done and learnt in relation to the learning objective. Teachers also might ask questions to the class to assess how far they have come in achieving the objective.[2] In current times, the given structure of a lesson is not as strictly determined. Thus, as the plenary is not a fixed requirement, it is often neglected. However, if teachers and school leaders are to take seriously the suggestion that authentic learning might include a process of reflection, it might mean that the plenary, or even the mini-plenaries that were once encouraged, might provide those moments in which learning experiences can have value beyond any immediate expectations, inspire agency and expediate change.

The womb and the mobius strip

The aspects of Bildung outlined above come some way to addressing the critique of dualism posed by Gillian Rose at the outset of this chapter. Bildung also underpins the proposition of a triune relation in which Spirit as the third partner in learning inspires creativity and new thinking in a middle space. Nevertheless, it might be argued that the educational shape outlined in Heimbrock's study, or the lesson on the playground are open to critique. Whilst the middle space between the self and world is the locus of new thinking, it might be suggested that this space itself is problematic.

In an editorial to the *International Journal of Children's Spirituality* by Hyde, Ota and Yust (2013), the middle space is illustrated in terms of a womb. Having distinct identities, the child and mother are in a unique relationship, one with the other (2013: 304). As the space between them, the womb provides the environment which is the locus of self-discovery. As provider of the space, the adult allows for the free development of the individual, but has a 'peripheral rather than central' role and contributes only when necessary (305). It might be argued however that since the child is the learner and the adult the provider, theory does not extend to accepting that the adult might also be a learner. The space allows for the child to be a part of the adult, yet the adult is not recognised in the child.

Whilst purporting to recognise the value of each partner, this idea is still adult-centric. As an allegory for education, this means that whilst learners are given agency, this takes place within the confines of an enclosed space. There is no breaking out or breaking through – rather formation within. It might be argued then that the mastery that Rose highlights as being detrimental to authentic learning is actually at play in this learning process. The learner is not open to self-examination in the light of the relation; yet neither is the provider. As such, mutual recognition is perpetuated and as much as the child eventually embarks on his or her own path of discovery through life, he or she will always carry the hallmarks of the parent. In the same way, as much as the student develops new ideas and thinking through creative interplay in the middle space, learning will always carry the hallmarks of the

dominant educational culture. This might mean that 'evidence' is col-
lected of such existential moments. This evidence might be uploaded
to the class photograph bank, displayed on the wall or written in a
'spirituality' book, for the perusal of inspectors during their next visit.
It also might mean that the 'personal learning' box might be ticked
before moving on to the next area of school life to be showcased.

In the light of the analogy of the womb, in this enclosed space of
mutual recognition, the educative *misrecognition* is not yet recognised.
The learning that results in the middle space is not interrupted and
not critiqued. This then carries the potential for such learning to become accepted as truth 'in-itself.' Learning becomes learning for itself.
This problematises any middle space in which new learning and understanding is not open to further scrutiny. As Nigel Tubbs asks: 'what
part can a teacher play in what appears to be an internal process?'
(2005: 221–222). Of course, we have established that in the relation of
self and other, both are important partners, but Tubbs' question raises
the question of ethics (and truth).

In both illustrations of Bildung, each learner or group of learners
experience the freedom and self-development of von Humboldtian
Bildung, but without any intervention from 'Other.' Such learning therefore has the potential to become fixed and as outlined in
Chapter 2, unethical. In reference to the outdoor games lesson, the responses of the children regarding teamwork were touching and inspi-
rational. Nevertheless, in the same situation and given the potentiality
offered for free thinking, some children might equally have reflected
on the downside of teamwork, in which slower runners impede the
progress of the others. This might allow them to problematise disability for instance and thus perpetuate a contrary idea to that which
was pre-supposed by the learning objective. Therefore, for the middle
space not to be enclosed, and the outcome of learning in this space not
to be objectified, there requires some re-negotiation.

Tubbs' proposition is to view the relation of self and other as a contradiction, and to recognise the educational value of this. He posits
that the student is no longer a servant *or* a master. He or she now has
a new status: servant *and* master. Thus, whilst a means-to-end performative approach to education is inadequate and inauthentic, that
through which interplay inspires the learner's own self-formation and
meaning-making is equally so. Ironically, and this is the contradiction, the learning relation requires intervention from a teacher. But
this teacher is not necessarily the adult at the front of the class. This
teacher (inspired as Spirit) is the means by which all learners (adult
and child alike) come to question both top-down and self-led learning,

to negate it and to recognise 'the part it plays in her own self-identity and its continual negation' (Tubbs 2005: 222).

This means that ethical Bildung involves doubt and questioning, risk and pain. It might be suggested then that in Heimbrock's study, the reworking of an image of God through Bildung, whilst having personal meaning for the learner, incites a risk to the host tradition. Yet when this learning itself is open to critique from a teacher in a different form, it can learn its own truth as a contradiction. This contradiction recognises the value of misrecognition.

When misrecognition is misrecognised (as in mutual recognition), or ignored, learning requires a resolution or difficulties are simply evaded. But when misrecognition is recognised, the unequal (triune) relational shape opens up the middle space. This space is not enclosed, such as in the analogy of the womb, but becomes the (unseen) domain in which learners can wrestle with their own personal understandings against the backdrop of those that are inherited or assumed. In this way, as suggested above, both self and other, and their relation, are significant partners in learning. Yet through the interruption of their necessary relation in misrecognition, what takes place in the middle space is also open to evaluation and critique, thus ensuring that learning is not fixed or perpetuated as a totality.

It might be argued here that in all cases, the identity of the learner and learning is at risk. Tubbs refers to this as groundlessness (2008: 87). This means that the priority of the dominant paradigm is groundless in its relation to other (either through interplay or critical reflection). But furthermore, the result of the learning relation is similarly groundless, in relation to the 'Otherness' which intervenes. Therefore, in the example provided at the beginning of this chapter, my position as class teacher, and the learning situation that I convened, became groundless in the light of the intervention of the child who became the 'teacher.' Going forward, the ideas that formed as a result of this intervention are similarly subject to groundlessness, being open to critique and re-evaluation, should they in turn become totalities or examples of learning 'in-itself.'

It must be noted that in posing a risk, or in inciting groundlessness, one is not choosing an easy path. In her book of the same name, Gillian Rose suggests that rather being enclosed, the middle space might be recognised as a 'broken middle.' Here the identification of a broken middle not only highlights the importance of self and other but also embraces the contradiction of their relation and thus the difficulties that result from it. She asserts that without process and pain, one cannot come to know (1992: xii). For Tubbs, 'the truth of learning is where the student learns about himself in relation to the teacher' (2008: 168). This learning takes place through contradiction and difficulty, and not through their overcoming. Therefore, when difficulties and contradictions are welcomed, and the teacher 'comes to know them differently, she can comprehend their truth in and as the philosophy of the teacher' (2005: 168).

The broken middle is another way of describing the interruption as outlined above. In visual terms, this might be illustrated through the image of a mobius strip. According to Lars Lovlie, a contemporary interpretation of Bildung is represented by a strip (usually of paper) that 'turns its inside out as it curves back on itself in a loop' (2003: 151). As a continuous connection between inside and outside, this dynamic representation of interplay intimates learning as an ongoing process with no fixed or end result. For Lovlie, Bildung's 'world' concerns temporality and history. He writes the 'recollection of history consists in seeing the old in the altered perspective of the present.' Thus history (or educational culture) in creative interplay is maintained (that is, not eschewed or undermined) but one's understanding of it is changed. He writes 'the existence that has been, now comes into being' (151) and this informs new understanding.

The mobius strip also inspires the interruption of interplay. As both sides of the strip will never be unified, neither will self and other be unified. The inability to unite thus ensures that any self-sufficient or uncritiqued learning that is inspired in the middle space is ultimately broken. It can never achieve the status of learning that is fully truthful as its truth lies in its brokenness. Thus, learning that is inspired through reflection or evaluation is truthful for the time at which it was formed. It must continue to evolve and change. Similarly, so does the learner or learning environment. As the mobius strip represents a paradox with no end, likewise it is paradoxical for the past and future to unite in continuous learning. Therefore, it involves the dynamic movement of reflexivity that also allows for the education and transformation of the present individual in the light of his or her existing educational culture. Similar to the 'broken middle,' the movement between the relational partners assures that each 'self' is constantly being reformed and re-imagined, and each learns of itself in a way that is unfixed and unstable.

The continuation of history, the development of the personal contingency of the learner and the evolving environment mean that this 'truth' will continue to develop and change. As much as this book is not about Theology or Religious Education, the ideas of Ana Maria Rizzuto are helpful in understanding this. Her idea of a middle ground created between two positions recognises and accepts the danger and tension already introduced. As a clinical researcher and practitioner in psychological and pastoral care, Rizzuto's research project *The birth of the living God* focuses on people's images of God. Grounded in the lives of patients who revealed concepts of God that changed and evolved according to their life experiences, she considers one's relationship with or image of God as a transitional object relation (Rizzuto 1979: 177). In this respect the truth of an image of 'God' lies in the space between the personal and the traditional.

In conclusion to an overview of Bildung then, it might be suggested that as the image or 'bild' is always in process, so too is its meaning. I posit that when Bildung becomes the end in itself, it needs to be reassessed. This means that when, for example, the term Bildung is commonly used as an alternate word for education, this promotes meaning in-itself. It cannot be a process pertaining to one-size-fits-all. When Bildung aspires to the totality of the learner through interplay or self-determination, it must be critiqued. Yet when Bildung is found in broken middle between the learner and the world, with its meaning provisional and outcomes unfixed, then it might have something to offer.

So, what does this mean for primary education? In relation to the proposition that pedagogy should include learning 'beyond the objective,' education as explored here concerns the development of the contingent self within the school context, over and above meeting targets. Continuing the theme of the self and other relation, interplay allows for the creation of a space – a learning dimension which, as a broken middle, transcends the immediate. Interplay in the process of Bildung recognises the value of external influences, such as the curriculum and learning objectives, but in relation with the self, their influence should not be total or fixed. This then might inspire a continuous learning process.

Having implications for history, geography, science, art, music and mathematics, amongst other curriculum areas, this view of Bildung allows for personal development and self-formation as well as the acquisition of knowledge and skills, as suggested, for example, by the National Curriculum framework for England. It might be argued that in the recognition of a middle space between the learner and curriculum, teachers can provide a platform for what Heimbrock calls 'playful interaction' (1999: 55). This transcends immediate learning, such as that which is transmitted and exists as a totality (for example, the presentation of historical narrative as fait accompli), and allows learners to question, think deeper and take their own development beyond that which is 'given.' Furthermore, when the broken middle is evident, attention is given to the role of criticality in the representation of what is learnt, and as a result what is understood becomes open to scrutiny, thus avoiding it becoming a totality.

In order to illustrate this in practice, I draw on an experience from several years ago, at a time when I was invited to model creative teaching methods in a school in Croatia. The students I taught were a largely Catholic group of secondary school students (aged 14), living not far from the capital Zagreb, a city which had in their lifetime (albeit when they were younger than school age), been the victim of the bomb attacks and fighting in the Yugoslavian civil war. Not far from the place in which we worked, disused buildings ruined by the bombs were a reminder of that horrific experience.

One activity involved composing a piece of music that represented war and peace. As contingent individuals with their own memories and impressions, they brought their own experiences to the activity. This included their memories of war, the stories told by family and their desire for peace. It is fair to say that this inspired emotional involvement as well as the cognitive or creative aspects of learning. As they brought their contingent selves to the music activity, the outcome of which was a requirement of their course, they were able to express how they felt about life in the present. As a result, due to their reflection in the middle space, learning went 'beyond the objective.' However, the over-riding feeling emanating from the students was fear and as the teacher, I reflected on how it was potentially unethical for this 'lesson' to draw out such feelings without any form of after care in place. Akin to the interruption which inspires the broken middle, following the activity, members of the group commented on their reflections and expressed how they were determined to address their own feelings towards war; together they suggested they might do this in their own time through discussion, art and prayer.

Repetition

The process of bringing historical and cultural experiences to learning is reminiscent of the process Repetition introduced in the book of the same name by nineteenth-century Danish thinker Soren Kierkegaard. In his illustration of Bildung as a mobius strip, Lars Lovlie likens the process also to Repetition, which he describes as providing the potential for the moment when 'the existence that has been, now comes into being' (Kierkegaard 1962: 131, cited in Lovlie 2003: 151). Recognising that education reveals untruth (or doubt), Nigel Tubbs describes Repetition as a process that 'repeats precisely the impossibility of a beginning that can be known only as unknown' (2005: 223). As such, Repetition involves the existence of the learner, and is involved in self-formation and understanding. Yet the twist (referred to above as the contradiction), is in the recognition that learning is not just about what is gained through educational experience. It is also about the negation of this learning – or as Tubbs suggests, doubt. This means that learning never becomes fixed or in-itself; it is always open to critique, re-evaluation and re-formation.

Before looking more closely at Repetition as a learning process, some background to Kierkegaard's life will be helpful in terms of illustrating his ideas. Soren Kierkegaard was born in Copenhagen, Denmark in 1813, to a dominant father and an illiterate mother (Gardiner 1998: 3). As a child he was physically weak but intellectually superior – the result of which left him often lonesome but yet contemplative, particularly regarding the domination of the Lutheran Faith to which his father subscribed (4). As such, his texts are often self-reflective, writing in the light of a number of personal issues, including the struggle and reconciliation with his father, and the difficulties inspired by his father's death. Loss was also a feature, reflecting his failure to be accepted into the Danish Church and most notably his broken engagement from Regina Olsen in 1841 (Collins 1983: 8–9). Gardiner suggests that Kierkegaard's troubles in no way hindered the progress of his literary career, and in fact, his broken engagement especially 'initiated a remarkable burst of activity' (1988: 11). As will be indicated in due course, this difficulty and loss might also play a part in the perspective of education proposed here.

One hallmark of his texts is his reticence to accept inherited knowledge of philosophical and theological ideas as truth, as was expected in his day (Gardiner 1988: 35–36). He wrestled with those who proposed epistemological certainty. Akin to what has been already suggested, he found truth in doubt and as Collins states, Kierkegaard 'had the courage to doubt all things but not to know and take possession of all things' (Collins 1983: 10). This is illustrated in his use of authorial pseudonyms. As he does not purport to be the author, the illusion created by each pseudonym disallows any claim to truth that he might promote, allowing readers to access and understand his writing on their own terms (Gardiner 1988: 44). As such, Kierkegaard's thesis is that any claim to understanding is really misunderstanding. For him, authentic learning involves a leap into the unknown: the leap of faith (Kierkegaard 1985: 53).

The book *Repetition* is written under the pseudonym Constantine Constantius and begins by highlighting the inadequacies of Socratic 'recollection.' In an earlier text, *Philosophical Fragments*, Kierkegaard had already explored Socrates' method of teaching and learning, described as an act of remembering (1974: 11). In this text, he notes that in recollection truth is drawn out from within the learner. The teacher acts as a midwife who leads the learner into the truth of his or her own knowing. The truth of the knower lies in questioning and the questioner is able to acquire the truth by recollecting and remembering (15). In *Repetition*, Kierkegaard highlights a deficiency regarding recollection, which pertains to the idea that truth is already present and as such there is no need for any occasion of learning, or intervention from a teacher. As there is no significant 'other,' there is no middle space. As a pedagogy based on questions, of which there is no answer outside of the self, learning is negative. As Tubbs points out, Socrates knows nothing, has nothing to teach and as an anti-master 'pulls the rug from under the feet of students and leaves them with nothing' (2005: 219). This is inadequate: an epistemological shortcoming that leads to unhappiness (Kierkegaard 2009: 3).

Repetition on the other hand might be described in colloquial terms as 'recollection plus.' Its significance is in its relational shape. Yet it is not just a relation of self and other, such as those critiqued earlier in this discussion. It is an unequal relation of self and other as past and future. It concerns not only what has gone, to be later drawn out from within as in recollection; it is also about what is to come. It is important to note that founded upon the contingent and historical, it is located within the 'world,' be this the environment, cultural context or even historical continuity. Yet it also relies on a revelation from the unknown future on the grounds of the condition provided by 'the teacher' in the present. In Repetition, 'that which has existed now comes into existence' (Kierkegaard 2009: 19). It is this revelation – the intervention from a significant 'other' that marks its diremption from recollection.

As has already been suggested, we might question who this 'teacher' or significant 'other' might be. This question pertains to one of the over-riding discussions in Philosophy of Education and is linked not only to the work of academics, but is also prevalent in the trajectory of educational theory and practice, which has seen much change over the three decades in which I have been involved in schools. In the primary school of course, each class has a designated teacher who constructs and maintains the learning environment, plans the lessons, and marks the children's work in order to provide feedback and formative assessment. The teacher also highlights how some children might benefit from 'intervention' and often such students will receive learning support in small groups or individually.

Yet in the light of the current discussion, the 'teacher' might also be another student and intervention might be of an existential rather than academic nature. In Repetition, the learner draws on one's prior understanding (of self), in the light of the cultural and historical world (other). When the condition (space) is opened in which learning might be developed through the interplay of self and other (Bildung), the 'teacher' is able to intervene, so learning is taken forward into an unknown future. In the light of this, learning cannot be fixed or claimed as truth, but is open to further evolution in the light of what the future holds.

As often in Kierkegaard's texts, a story provides an allegory for his philosophical thinking. Published in 1843, *Repetition* concerns the plight of a man in love with a young girl. It tracks his journey from knowing the girl 'ideally,' that is admiring her from afar, to knowing her in actuality. Whilst not yet in a relationship with her, the man is able to recollect how he feels, drawing on his capacity to love. But the movement is only within him and does not extend to expressing his love to her. This causes him unrest as it concerns the contradiction of loving and not having. With this comes unhappiness. The author stresses that this man is far from realising this ideal love due to his 'melancholy soul' (Kierkegaard 2009: 48). For his own education, the young man requires Repetition to understand who he is in relation to the girl and to gain clarity regarding his intent (49). He recognises that although they have never met, she is the one who allows him to understand himself more fully in the present in order to inform the future.

Through the contradiction, he becomes aware that this unequal relation is the beginning of his education (Kierkegaard 2009: 93). The paradox of ideality and actuality is indeed his learning tool. In the author's commentary on the situation of the young man, Kierkegaard as Constantius explains that whilst the girl does not have actuality, it is not she as herself that is significant. The relation the young man has with her, albeit ideal, is that which illuminates who he really is. He comes to learn about himself in an ideal relation to her. She is his teacher: the one who brings him to learn from his situation. Kierkegaard writes: 'the girl has not actuality but is simply a reflection of, and occasion for, movements within him' (49).

This educative movement is Repetition. The relation between what is recollected (ideally his innate love) and the girl in actuality is unequal; it is a mis-relation. In the movement of Repetition, the relationship of self and other will not be reconciled (Tubbs 2004: 86–87): the young man wishes to break away from this affair. It is too difficult. Yet in the space between ideality and actuality, the young man experiences the learning of his own truth through reflection on his torment. As such the triadic learning shape keeps this relation open, and in the middle space, the girl intervenes, to become his teacher and allow him to develop self-understanding.

For the young man, the significance of his learning is not his possession of the girl, but his understanding gained through loss. Tubbs notes that what is possessed can only be gained in the educational significance of it being lost. He writes: 'gaining or receiving is learning that possession, loss and gain are the absolute relation of recollection and repetition' (Tubbs 2004: 93). Loss for the young man involves not only negating the reality of the girl, but also negating his immediate self. This is manifest in the rupture (interruption) of self-sufficiency (Kierkegaard 2009: 59); through this rupture, the young man recognised the contradiction of his relation with the girl. In the middle space he was able to re-evaluate and re-learn what had been already understood, and this inspired new understanding to be taken forward.

An illustration of this is provided by a creative activity that took place not in the classroom but on a family holiday. Whilst not pertaining strictly to the formal learning environment, learning such as is described here might have taken place in any setting.

In May 2017, 22 people were killed in a suicide bombing at a concert at the Manchester Arena (U.K). In the Summer that followed, on a holiday afternoon at the beach, a family which includes three children aged 5 to 10, engaged in a moment of Repetition to create a symbol of remembrance and hope. Wanting to create a memorial to the lost, using stones and shells they created a picture of a bee, which historically is the symbol of Manchester.[3] Along the top they wrote the motto 'And the bees still buzz.' Photos were taken of this image and as well as being shared on social media, they were used as a resource in school R.E. lessons. In fact, one picture became the 'face' of the website of a business local to the beach.

As a side-note, the symbol of the bee represents the industrial history of the city of Manchester. As a major site of the Industrial Revolution in nineteenth-century Great Britain, many of the population worked in mills and factories, and were commonly referred to as 'busy bees.' This sense of duty and work instilled a sense of strength and unity in the people of the city, and it does to this day.

As in Repetition, the family began by recollecting their own previous personal experiences of loss. In so doing they were able to feel empathy for those who had lost loved ones and in drawing on these feelings they became inspired to show solidarity. In the middle space between their own contingent feelings and experiences and the natural world around them, they created something unique. In so doing, they reflected on the horrors of the atrocity. Yet furthermore, as the picture emerged, they were able consider hope for a better future and the motto highlighted how the drive for respect and equality intensified in the lives of these children.

Having been shared on social media, the picture has now become an icon of hope. In this case we might say that it represents the 'teacher' who illuminates this sense of hope. Through engaging with this image, the viewer becomes the means by which any meaning created is prevented from becoming a totality. In his or her own engagement with the image, further learning, with the potentiality for deeper or different meanings, ensures the continuity of the learning process. This is taken forward into the future, not as a fixed understanding but, like the mobius strip, as a contradiction in which the past and present meet for a re-imagined future.

Bildung's Repetition

The relation of interplay and repetition leads then to the conclusion of the philosophical section of this book. This presents what might be described as a relation of relation, which here I now refer to as 'Bildung's Repetition.' As a working title, 'Bildung's Repetition' is termed as such in the respect that it encompasses the two educational processes explored here. For the primary school, I would probably use different terminology such as 'creative reflection' or 'learning for the future,' or indeed, to quote the title of this book, 'learning beyond the objective.' But in a sense, any form of label might signify an intended outcome, which is of course antithetical to the premise outlined above. Therefore, when teachers or school leaders consider how this perspective might be inspired in school, it is worth noting that we are not looking at models or schemes which are fixed entities. Rather we are concerned with promoting a vision for embracing the learning that might be unseen or uncovered, yet contains existential potential for each individual.

So, what does this mean for the primary school? Here are a few points for practitioners and leaders to consider. Any learner (adult or child) brings his or her own history to the learning process. This is referred to in this text as contingency and must be recognised. No learner lives or learns in a vacuum and so the system of learning, or even the learning environment, be it the classroom, nursery school, after-school club or home and the sub-structure within this environment, such as the curriculum or lesson, meet with the contingent individual for his or her education. This is not a relation of power in which one has control over the other; yet it is not a necessary relation, or an example of mutual recognition. Rather it is unequal, signified by a middle space which is opened when the learner and other (system/structure) relate in an informative way. This is described here as an interplay, otherwise known as Bildung. Within this interplay, creative reflection allows each individual to draw on his or her contingency in order to make a response. This response might include questioning, critical intervention or doubt, but in each case, it illuminates new ideas in the present, so to inform new meanings for the future.

'Bildung's Repetition' can be outworked in practice when learners are given the opportunity to make personal responses to the curriculum in an environment which inspires reflection and the further development of thinking. Of course, it is much more obvious to allow children to respond to literary texts, works of art or even their own or others' creative writing. Yet it is argued here that in the more technocratic subjects such as mathematics, science and even modern foreign languages, a perspective that is aware of and caters for the dimension beyond the objective can allow for meaningful learning over and above that which is measured or assessed. A more robust appraisal of how this learning perspective might be applied in the classroom is provided in the following chapter.

In summarising this perspective, I suggest that the meanings developed by learners in the middle space of interplay have significance for their personal lives. This learning is authentic. Yet it is important that teachers and learners recognise that these meanings are provisional. Thus, such meanings must again be suspended, so to continue the process of learning. As it persists throughout the life of the learner or even the educational environment, Bildung's Repetition enables the revision of learning, continuing to shape individuals and communities, and it is hoped, ultimately, transform.

Notes

1 See https://plato.stanford.edu/entries/wilhelm-humboldt/#RetuGermPubl EducPoli accessed 10 January 2019.
2 See https://www.theschoolrun.com/what-is-a-learning-objective accessed 16 December 2018.
3 See http://www.manchestereveningnews.co.uk/news/greater-manchester-news/manchester-bee-meaning-symbol-why-13112437 accessed 4 September 2017.

References

Buber, M. (1970), *I and Thou*, New York: Charles Scribner's Sons.
Collins, J. (1983), *The Mind of Kierkegaard*, Princeton: Princeton University Press.

Freire, P. (1996), *Pedagogy of the Oppressed*, London: Penguin.

Gardiner, P. (1988), *Kierkegaard: A Very Short Introduction*, Oxford: Oxford University Press.

Gunther-Heimbrock, H. (1999), 'Images and pictures of God: creative ways of seeing,' in *International Journal of Children's Spirituality*, 4, No. 1. 51–60.

Hegel, G. (1977), *Phenomenology of Spirit*, Oxford: Oxford University Press.

Heidegger, M. (1962), *Being and Time*, Oxford: Blackwell.

Hyde, B. (2010), 'Agency, play and spiritual development in the early years' curriculum,' in *Meaning and Connectedness: Australian Perspectives on Education and Spirituality*, de Souza, M., and Rimes, J. (eds), Australia: Australian College of Educators.

Hyde, B., Ota, C., and Yust, K.M. (2013), 'Wombing: chorionic companions, amniotic accompaniers and placental partners,' in *International Journal of Children's Spirituality*, 18, No. 4. 303–305.

Kierkegaard, S. (1974), *Philosophical Fragments*, Princeton: Princeton University Press.

Kierkegaard, S. (1985), *Fear and Trembling*, Chichester: Princeton University Press.

Kierkegaard, S. (2009), *Repetition and Philosophical Crumbs*, Oxford: Oxford University Press.

Levinas, E. (2003), *Totality and Infinity*, Pittsburgh: Duquesne University Press.

Lovlie, L. (2003), 'The promise of bildung,' in Lovlie, L., Mortensen, K.P., and Nordenbo, S.E. (eds), *Educating Humanity: Bildung in Postmodernity*, Oxford: Blackwell.

Lovlie, L., and Standish, P. (2003), 'Introduction,' in Lovlie, L., Mortensen, K.P., and Nordenbo, S.E. (eds), *Educating Humanity: Bildung in Postmodernity*, Oxford: Blackwell.

Nordenbo, S.E. (2003), 'Bildung and the thinking of bildung,' in Lovlie, L., Mortensen, K.P., and Nordenbo, S.E. (eds), *Educating Humanity: Bildung in Postmodernity*, Oxford: Blackwell.

Pridmore, J. (2004), 'Dancing cannot start too soon,' in *International Journal of Children's Spirituality*, 9, No. 3. 279–291.

Reynaert, M. (2014), 'Pastoral power in nurturing the spiritual life of the child,' in *International Journal of Children's Spirituality*, 19, No. 3–4. 179–186.

Rizzuto, A.M. (1979), *The Birth of the Living God*, Chicago: Chicago University Press.

Rose, G. (1992), *The Broken Middle*, Oxford: Blackwell.

Rose, G. (1996), *Mourning Becomes the Law*, Cambridge: Cambridge University Press.

Tubbs, N. (2004), *Philosophy's Higher Education*, Dordrecht: Kluwer Academic Publishers.

Tubbs, N. (2005), *The Philosophy of the Teacher*, Oxford: Blackwell.

Tubbs, N. (2008), *Education in Hegel*, London: Continuum Books.

von Humboldt, W. (2000), 'Theory of Bildung,' in Westbury, I., Hopmann, S., and Riquarts, K. (eds), *Teaching as a Reflective Practice*, London: Lawrence Erlbaum.

4 An existential perspective for the curriculum

Summary

This book opened with the suggestion that education in primary schools in a UK context and in other global situations might be described as performative. This means that due to external motivators such as the publication of examination results, and the league tables that are subsequently formed based on these results, teaching often adopts a means-to-end perspective. Here, success is measured on the children's ability to perform according to an externally agreed set of standards and requirements. This is further exacerbated by formal inspection systems that require evidence of rigorous learning throughout the school. Inspections also involve observing and evaluating the work of teachers and leaders, assessing data pertaining to student attainment and scrutinising pupil progress.

In Chapter 1, it was highlighted through studies and reports from countries such as Australia, Hong Kong and Norway, that this educational culture has had an impact on not only student well-being and mental health but also on that of the class teacher. In the studies represented, teachers noted the tension they felt between their personal objectives for teaching and the requirements from Governments. For some it became clear that the balance of power in schools erred towards the externally driven motivators and away from the inner life of each learner. This power relation was described in the early chapters as mastery, and it seems that all participants in education are slaves to its demands.

Having identified the etymology of education as the Latin term 'educare,' which symbolises a drawing out of learning from each individual's experiences, the framework for the Early Years Foundation Stage of education in England (from age 3 to 5) was noted as being more closely related to the 'ideal' of 'educare' in terms of its emphasis on developing creativity and imagination through child-led learning within enabling environments. However, on entering the first of four 'Key Stages' at age 5–6, children quickly realise that they must adapt to a different kind of access to learning, including sitting at desks, writing in books and taking tests. It must be noted here that the opportunity for learning through play or creativity, both in the indoor and outdoor environment is still a requirement for all children in Key Stage One. However, these sessions are accompanied by more formal learning activities, with given outcomes and success criteria.

According to McDowall Clark (2016: 41), the change in rhetoric from 'framework' to 'key stage' is indicative of the change in educational structure that the children experience, with the suggestion of scaffolded yet child-led learning taking place within the *framework*, and the more adult-led learning which is structured and assessed, taking place in the more formally constructed *stage*.

One means of assessing pupil progress at least for the short term is the learning objective. In Chapter 1, the learning objective was highlighted as the means by which adults and children in classes might identify success in learning, as well as ensuring that lessons meet the demands of the prescribed curriculum. Turning to the idea of mastery again, the dominant force in the learning experience is the requirement to meet the objective; success thus pertains to how well the criteria is fulfilled. In Chapter 2, it was noted that the existence of the Being of the learner is also a significant factor in learning and that when this dimension of personhood is acknowledged, mastery can be overcome.

However, as already stated, it is not the purpose of this book to negate global education systems or structures, or to propose a new *paradigm* of education. This would be unethical and wrong. What is proposed here is a new perspective that embraces both the macro-education system, identified in micro-terms in the learning objective, *in relation with* the Being or existence of the learner. This is not a dualistic relation but a renegotiated relation which is imbalanced and broken. The imbalance here results from an interruption. The new perspective proposed in this book, termed philosophically as Bildung's Repetition, recognises this unequal relation of self and other and aspires to recognise the learning that takes place in a middle space between the two. In adopting this perspective, which involves not much more than a ten-degree shift, practitioners might offer the potential for an education that while meeting set objectives within curricula, also goes beyond.

In the light of my role as a teacher in a primary school, a number of teaching and learning sessions that I have facilitated over many years have highlighted this perspective. In the current chapter, drawing on case studies and some empirical data, it is outlined how the curriculum, or the set subjects for study might provide opportunities for the creation of the space in which learning beyond the objective can take place. Ideas for promoting an existential perspective through history, writing, geography, art and drama, mathematics and music are outlined. Additional material considers the existential aspect of cross-curricular activities, so that teachers and headteachers might begin to recognise the value of embracing an existential dimension of learning in whole school life.

Case studies – history and writing

A number of years ago, the topic for Class Six (children aged 10–11) in the Summer term was 'Heroes.' As I taught this class for one afternoon per week, I decided to choose a small number of significant people from the past 100 years and focus on one in each session. The overall learning objective for these lessons was taken from the curriculum documents for history produced by the Local Education Authority. The overall objective, shared with the children at the start of each lesson was: 'We are learning to understand the achievements of mankind.' Each individual lesson however had its own objective relevant to its curriculum focus.

One lesson focused on Rosa Parks and her role in the Civil Rights Movement in America in 1955.

Rosa Parks was a young African-American woman who refused to give up her seat on a Montgomery to Alabama bus, to make room for white passengers when the bus driver ordered her to. She was arrested but her act of defiance was one of the events to inspire the Civil Rights Movement in America.

The class had already learnt about Martin Luther King's march from Selma to Washington DC, and so had previous learning upon which to draw. Having invited the children to write a first-person diary account of the event, they were keen to put themselves in the metaphorical shoes of this amazing young girl and consider her story from a personal perspective. At the end of the lesson, children were given the opportunity to share their work with the class. As the sharing took place, in response one child began to cry. She had been emotionally affected by this story and stated that we should never let oppression happen in this way again. This led to verbal responses from other children, for example, from one boy who asked the existential question of why oppression exists, and another who asked what can be done to help those who suffer. A further child led the way in providing an answer to the questions and suggested that the whole class should begin by talking to people at home about identity – encouraging them to accept all peoples, regardless of difference.

As a heart-warming example of Bildung's Repetition, we can see here how the authentic education of those children was that which stirred them into questioning, reflecting and choosing to make a change. So, what happened? If we draw parallels with the different aspects of Bildung's Repetition we can first identify that both self and other were involved in this act of learning. The contingent existence of the learners, when drawing on previous historical knowledge and their own perceptions of discrimination, was brought to the learning situation provided by the 'other' here represented by the framework for history and subsequently the story. In the middle space between the two, through the writing and listening, the children were able to reflect on the story in the light of their own recollections.

It might be argued that this not a new idea in education. Some teachers might suggest that examples such as this happen regularly in their classrooms. Nevertheless, what might be considered here as new is the question: *who is the teacher*? In Bildung's Repetition, what is significant is the intervention that interrupts what is created in the middle space, resulting in the unequal relational shape. This interruption allows the learning to go in a different, yet more challenging direction. In the light of this illustration, we might consider that the 'teacher' was indeed the child who asked the critical questions; the key learning of the session therefore was not the understanding of the achievement of mankind per se, but the suggestion offered by the third child, that we all might play a part in encouraging acceptance of difference. As a learning outcome, this was not in any way intended or planned for. Yet the condition for learning, which provided the potential for going beyond the objective, gave the children the opportunity to create new and authentic meanings, which it is hoped will continue to have an impact on them on both a personal level and indeed wider.

A further example comes from a different class in the same school. The class topic was World War II and the children had followed the story of Anne Frank on a DVD. Anne Frank was a German-born Jewish teenager living in Amsterdam during the period of World War II. She and her family were hidden in the attic of a downtown house for two years before being found and arrested. During her time in hiding she wrote a diary, which was subsequently found and published in 1947. Anne died in Bergen-Belsen concentration camp in 1945.

Having done some personal research about the story of Anne Frank, I discovered that soon after the publication of her diary, a number of adaptations were produced for the stage and screen including one theatre show named 'And then they came for me.'[1] In class, after revisiting the end of the story as depicted on film, the children were given a small strip of paper and 15 minutes, and again invited to write a short first-person account of the story, drawing on own their feelings and responses to the situation. As a writing lesson, the secondary learning objective stated 'We are learning to use powerful words in writing.' The children were told that their success would depend on their use of similes, emotion words and noun phrases. This indeed was the case, but the wider outcome of the lesson revealed much more in the way of existence.

Following the writing, the children were invited to share their work with the class. A number of children volunteered and as each one read, the class was reduced to silence. Looking uncomfortable and visibly moved, many of the children began to drift into their own worlds of thought and began to reflect on the sad situation represented in each personal account. As the bell rang for play time, it seemed as it if would be wrong to leave what had become a sort of 'sacred space.' Whilst of course not being a religious space, there was something tangible yet unarticulated about the sharing of the readings that had brought the children together in a special, spiritual way. Quietly I explained that play time was optional and that if staying in class was important to them, they could stay and I would be there. The children did leave, but in their own time, quietly and respectfully.

It is fair to say that as a writing activity, the children's work was marked and evaluated according to the criteria determined by the learning objective. As usual in a writing task they were given the opportunity to revise their writing before typing out on the computer or writing up as a final draft in their books. Yet, in the moment described above, when such significant learning took place, to refer back to the objective in the class setting, to ask them for their own self-evaluations, or even to provide the plenary that ensures that they have met the criteria for success, would have been to undermine the significance of the moment. Thus, the lesson ended quietly on the children's own terms. The impact of the learning was extended further when some of the children read their stories to parents and the wider school in a celebration assembly. Again, a special moment was created. Visitors were visibly moved, and one parent was prompted to send an e-mail to the Headteacher indicating how the stories had reminded her of the need to engage with the past so that the future might be different.

In reflection on this case study, we might suggest as above that the contingent existence of the learners, in interplay with the historical situation, allowed for creative inter-subjectivity in the present. Yet further, Bildung's Repetition inspired the interruption of regular learning through the spontaneous creation of a sacred space. This interruption opened up a dimension of learning that took the children beyond the simple use of 'powerful words.' In turn, it inspired a moment of illumination, this time for the visitors in assembly, taking the learning forward and into the future. Once more, as the facilitator of this task, I was not the teacher that gave the participants this special moment. As the condition for the potential of personal learning was offered, the real, or authentic dimension of this lesson was that brought to the children's inner selves. As new learning, it was taken forward not as a totality but as the inspiration for further reflection.

With permission, an example of the children's writing is presented here.

And then they came for me. Silence filled the room. My mother had her hand over my mouth as we sat deadly still in the corner. They were coming for us. The door slammed open and I began to shake like a dog. My mother screamed and my father shouted to me over and over again 'RUN, RUN, RUN!' I ran towards the door, tears racing down my face. A blinding torch light stopped me dead in my tracks. The cold end of a gun pressed against my back. I was drowning in fear. Pain stabbed through my body as I fell to the floor. I could not feel my knees. I heard one last scream as I felt my head against the cold, hard floor.

It might be argued that the two examples here relate to emotionally charged stories that might influence children in a way that such personal responses would inevitably be made. It might also be argued that the learning situations were manipulative, thus raising ethical questions. These are fair suggestions and must be taken into consideration. And not every lesson of course will have an existential outcome. As indicated in the philosophical discussion in this book, it would be an inauthentic teacher who prepares in advance for the more personal outcomes. Nevertheless, as these two case studies indicate, Bildung's Repetition highlights how teachers might recognise that education involves more than meeting set targets. When we create the conditions in our classrooms and lessons for the recognition of this extra dimension of learning, the learning objective becomes not only the criteria for assessment and ultimately success but also the catalyst for meaningful education.

Therefore, even the more pragmatic aspects of history might lend themselves to learning beyond. In learning how culture has changed over time, and in asking questions about how change has happened, children can position themselves in history and consider themselves as change-makers. In constructing ideas from the past from a range of sources, they can evaluate the impact of the present on the future, and in exploring life in early civilisations, such as Ancient Greece or Ancient Rome, they can consider the role of legacy, again looking to the future that they can help to shape.

In terms of writing, whilst drawing on the requirements for good composition such as the use of adverbials, conjunctions and prepositions, having the opportunity to write for a range of purposes, 'pupils can be encouraged to adopt, create and sustain a range of roles, responding appropriately to others in role.'[2] This might include writing persuasive letters of complaint to the local council, composing leaflets promoting recycling or healthy eating, or constructing poems highlighting the perils of global warming, all of which are regular activities in a primary school classroom. As much as these activities will help the children to achieve success in their end of year assessments, they also provide learners with the opportunity to bring their previous personal recollections to their learning experiences in the present, so to inspire a new and transformed future.

Case study – geography, art and drama

A number of years ago, I led a series of morning sessions with a class of children aged 8 in an urban primary school. The theme of the sessions was 'Water' and the aim was to provide a cross-curricular, integrated approach to the theme.[3] Although I was given the autonomy to devise my own activities within the lessons, observance of the National Curriculum was still required and each lesson had a learning objective.

A first port of call was a session based on the Water Cycle. Drawing on the guidelines for geography from the Local Authority, the children first explored the different aspects of the water cycle from the perspective of what is termed 'physical geography.' Using diagrams and differentiated writing approaches,[4] the children re-presented the cycle in their own terms. Following the lesson, one child highlighted that the water cycle is a way of recycling, and the class were able make connections between this ongoing natural phenomenon and their own actions.

Still having physical geography as a focus, the cross-curricular nature of the sessions opened out to a more creative approach. Thus, two art sessions followed. Both sessions were designed so that children would have the opportunity to 'explore' water, in terms of the objective 'we are learning to experiment with different effects and textures.' A number of activity stations were set up in the classroom; each activity was open-ended and allowed the children to use their imaginations as they experimented with texture and touch. In session one, after listening to the piano piece 'Reflects dans l'eau,' translated 'Reflections in the water,' by the nineteenth-century French composer Debussy, and being invited to imagine the ongoing movement in the water cycle, the children engaged in creative activities such as using acrylic paints on canvas, water colours on paper, chalks on card and mixing poster paints with sand (using their fingers, combs, toothbrushes and other media for effects) before painting on big boards. Other children searched through water images found on the internet and some created a PowerPoint presentation to express the different parts of the water cycle.

In the second session, the children first listened to the orchestral piece 'La Mer,' translated 'The Sea,' also by Debussy. This time the whole class sat around a long strip of thick paper and were given chalks, pastels and coloured pencils. They were invited to create shapes, shades and tones using the media provided in order to represent the movement of the water as portrayed by the music.

Following the first session, this conversation took place between myself and one of the children:

CHILD: *I love this lesson. I want it all the time coz it's fun.*
TEACHER: How is it fun?
CHILD: *You make a mess.*
TEACHER: Just a mess?
CHILD: *No, we made a water picture. I liked putting my hands in the paint and sand.*
TEACHER: What will your mum say when you go home with dirty hands?
CHILD: *She won't mind. She likes me to have fun at school.*

The child in the quote above obviously benefitted from being allowed to experiment freely with the media. I once heard a lecturer from a local college talk on a teacher training day about the power of the pigment. Having instilled this impression on the delegates, he encouraged teachers to consider the value of art for learners, suggesting that in creativity, the immediate dimension of reality gives way to something beyond consciousness. He suggested that this is where one finds one's own truth.

This assertion is supported by scholars in the field of Children's Spirituality, including Jaqueline Watson who, in reference to the notion of Bildung which she describes as 'an openness to other' (2013: 126), suggests that bodily or corporeal experiences allow for 'identity formation and transformation to occur' (127). She continues to note that Bildung's reflexive engagement with 'other' which includes 'a special source of truth' and 'mysterious ambiguity' (Gadamer 2011, cited in Watson 2013: 127), inspires the creation of a space in which a learner's existential identity might be recognised and re-formed. She writes: 'Spiritual pedagogy must involve space for a listening encounter with other; for children to encounter themselves and reflexively engage with other' (2013: 127). This of course is resonant with the current discussion and illuminates how corporeal experiences might inspire learning which is greater than that determined by set objectives.

Brendan Hyde also considers the significance of corporeality in learning, but focuses rather on the ontological dimension of bodily experiences. He likens the children's absorption in the activity to a oneness felt when being unified with other. He names this 'ontological awareness,' and it is his assertion that when one learns with one's whole self – mind, body and soul – an 'integration of the whole person with the whole experience' (2008: 89) takes place. This results in 'knowing' of a different kind – not the cognitive, empirical knowledge of curricula and tests, but holistic knowledge that as trans-cognitive, is just as significant (89–90).

Hyde also highlights how bodily experiences reflect a phenomenon described as 'flow' (2018: 84). This is the act of 'being involved' with an activity to the point that it seems to manage itself. The concept of flow was introduced by the social psychologist Mihaly Csikszentmihalyi (1990) who discovered that children involved in his research, when totally immersed in an activity, had an intensity and immediacy in the present moment (1990: 4). This led to the creation of meanings deeper than those prescribed, illustrated by the responses of the children in my lessons who commented on how the final products were almost created 'by magic' and how their finished pieces of work make them think 'wow' about the power of water in the natural world.

In the final session that I led in school, the focus changed from physical to human geography, linking to the wider objective of learning about the global distribution of natural resources (including water). Drama provided the tool for exploration. This session began with a mime activity where the children explored their own uses of water, such as cleaning their teeth, washing and drinking. They quickly identified how access to clean water is something taken for granted and they wanted to know more. I therefore retold a story about a boy called Moses who, living in Uganda, walked for several miles each day to obtain clean water. They saw pictures of Moses carrying a billy can, and were able to see the difficult terrains and weather conditions that he needed to negotiate as part of this daily task.

This led to an empathetic drama activity, in which the children imagined they were 'Moses,' walking each day to collect water in a billy can. They worked in groups and first engaged in a time of discussion and reflection about what life would be like before improvising, devising, rehearsing and sharing their short plays. As the children performed to each other, it became clear that the empathetic nature of the activity was having an impact on them personally. Following the performances, children responded using rhetoric such as 'it's not fair' and 'we couldn't do that'; one child stated how she would try to make a difference in the light of the session:

I have learned you can recycle, reuse and reduce things. You can even save water for later, just don't throw it down the sink.

In terms of Bildung's Repetition, each activity demonstrated how the interplay of self and other opened the space for reflection that allowed for transformation in the future. It might be argued however that, such as in the illustration of the womb critiqued in Chapter 3, the space in each of these examples is enclosed. When learning pertains to wholeness and the integration of self and other, there is no 'teacher' who intervenes. Nevertheless, the reflexivity highlighted by Watson, and the holistic knowing cited by Hyde both indicate how 'new' learning interrupts the prescription set in the learning objectives. The interruption, which inspires learning that goes deeper than and beyond the set curriculum, provides the opportunity for learning to be taken forward, and wider, to others.

This involves a sharing of responsibility and a collective sense of how actions on a local level might affect the well-being of others on a national or even international level. Richard Woolley in the co-authored text *The Spiritual dimension of Childhood* writes:

They (children) need to consider the impact of their choices and use of resources. Achieving this is the challenge for the effective development of skills necessary to become global citizens: it enables children to consider their interrelatedness with other people and their environment.

(Adams, Hyde and Woolley 2008: 105)

It might be argued that it is the creative aspects of the curriculum that lend themselves more naturally to interplay and therefore reflection on learning. This of course is true, illustrated by the use of drawings in the work of Heimbrock outlined earlier. Nevertheless, the more pragmatic aspects of geography might also lend themselves to learning beyond. In learning how to identify countries and continents on a map, and describing different weather patterns across the globe, students can consider the impact of their own actions on others. In asking questions about the importance of features such as wind farms and power stations, they can develop a sense of ecological ethics, and in describing contrasting cultures, they can become aware of themselves as global citizens. Bildung's Repetition therefore offers the opportunity for children and staff to evaluate their attitudes, beliefs and behaviours.

Case studies – music and mathematics

When I was growing up, many of my teachers would argue that mathematics and music went together hand in hand. As a relatively competent musician, but a poor student of mathematics, I often doubted this proposition. To me, music was a subject that made me feel inspired and empowered and most of all it was fun. Maths was just boring. However, as an adult and now a teacher it is possible to see the link between the two subjects, not least from an existential point of view. As such they go together in these final two case studies.

My consideration of the existential dimension of mathematics takes me back to my days as a student teacher. At the time, my reflections on pedagogy were not rooted in philosophy, and of course the notion of Bildung's Repetition was far from my thinking. Nevertheless, being allowed to work in an open-ended way, the ten weeks of my final placement in a wonderful small village school in England provided me with many opportunities to assess the relation of the learner to learning, rather than focusing on prescribed outcomes. This took place a couple of years before the introduction of the National Curriculum in England and Wales, and before testing as we experience it now became statutory. Therefore, I was allowed to devise my own scheme of work based on a topic of my choice. The topic I chose was Space.

It is important to remember that maths is not just about numbers – it is also about patterns and shape. Therefore, linking maths to the topic of Space, I provided the children with activities that represented 'space' in its widest sense. There were no learning objectives as such for the lessons, but in each case, the activities were designed to provide the students with a wider understanding of the topic. The children explored measurement through making three dimensional models, including a dodecahedron (with 12 sides). They investigated the impact of gravity and acceleration on the space shuttle's descent to earth, and lessons also involved number sequences and patterns. The children were amazed particularly at the Fibonacci sequence,[5] and at how its ongoing pattern created a spiral-like effect. One child, on writing out the Fibonacci sequence exclaimed: 'Miss Wills, it's beautiful!'

In the school, the staff and children had very comfortable relationships with each other, and within a culture of respect, the children were often given the opportunity to share their thoughts on their learning experiences. As a result, the personal impact of learning on the children was made evident to me in their informal conversations. It emerged that what impressed the children about the lessons the most was the precise nature of the numbers or patterns in relation to each other. A dodecahedron requires accurate measurements that match up. Imprecise measurements, evidenced by a number of failed attempts at construction, result in an imperfect shape. The rate of acceleration of an object when being moved by gravity must be precise to prevent disaster. The beauty of the number sequences also reflects the beauty of the stars, their location being determined by a string of equations that take us back into the past whilst providing light in the present.

Expressions such as 'it all fits together' and 'how is it so clever?' lead us to consider that the children in their responses to the activities were able to move from a pragmatic experience of mathematics and science, to one which inspired what might be regarded as a spiritually existential response. Bildung's Repetition demonstrates how the space for reflection and opportunity for discussion disallowed the lessons from being entities in themselves. Rather, the learning was taken forward to consider a dimension of life wider than the self, to wonder at the intricacies of the universe, and to reflect on one's own place in the world.

The literature of children's spirituality highlights the existential dimension of learning especially in relation to space and nature. For example, British scholars David Hay and Rebecca Nye in their seminal text *The Spirit of the Child*, reflect on the idea of mystery sensing, in which 'a consideration of the vastness of the universe strikes awe in us' (2006: 71). This consideration can provide moments where children exclaim 'it's beautiful' or learners can be encouraged to wonder. Often this is referred to as the 'wow' factor that can take us away from a paradigm of explanation, to one of mystery – in which learners can appreciate the unexplained (72). This can be a 'jolt to the system' of classifying and quantifying information (71) and opens up the potential for responses to the world that have no limits. In reference to his own empirical research study, Brendan Hyde highlights how his participants, children of primary school age, were able to 'draw upon their sense of wonder in order to make meaning of events and piece together a world view based around their attempts at meaning making' (2008: 108).

Continuous with this and from a philosophical perspective, Scott Webster argues that learning must be located in an existential framework. In a journal article from 2004, he explains how existential education should not only involve a learner's knowledge of objects or things, that is ideas or facts, but rather inspire a relationship with them, so that further learning might evolve. This is a familiar idea. In Bildung's Repetition, in the space created between the learner and the objects of learning, the agency or subjectivity of the learner develops his or her own meaning (2004: 13). In respect of the current case study, this led to an awareness of the intricacy of the universe. Yet for Webster, it does not end there. Even further learning is inspired, which includes the questions 'who am I?' or 'what am I?' and 'why am I here?' In this case, the learning which has already taken the students beyond the immediate is interrupted by the deep questions of existence which confront their own Being and purpose. These questions compel them to think more widely about their place in the world. This certainly goes way beyond the requirements of the curriculum, and whilst this learning doesn't promote any claim to objective truth regarding religion or even science, it does as Webster suggests, allow learners to consider their relation to the world and that which is beyond (14).

It might be argued that it is not the role of the primary teacher to encourage questions about the meaning of life, especially the teacher who requires his or her students to attain high marks in national tests. It also might be argued again that an ethical issue is presented here. When such deep questions are provoked without teachers having the time or space to devote to exploring their implications, does this equate to irresponsible teaching? Of course, it is the role of the teacher to ensure that the children are equipped to participate successfully in tests and have the necessary skills for life. Nevertheless, this case study reveals the capacity that children have for deep thinking, and in line with the aim of this book, it illuminates the potential that the curriculum holds for learning that is personal, meaningful and hopefully long-lasting. In the concluding chapter, it will be outlined how the Government, school leaders and teachers might provide for the learning as described here whilst still ensuring that curriculum aims are met.

The idea of patterns and shape in mathematics takes us to the final example of 'learning beyond the objective.' As a music specialist, it is easier for me to write about this subject than any other. Of course, as suggested above, the emotional aspect of music, with its links to story and songs and thus powerful political messages, invite learning beyond the immediate. However, here I hope to address the more relational aspect of curriculum music through a case study from a multi-ethic school in England.

As a visiting teacher to this school, I undertook a piece of research with a class of 8-year-old children. Some children represented the Hindu, Muslim, Christian and Sikh religions, and some were from the Afro-Caribbean culture. In the school, in line with the Local Education Authority's provision of a 'determination,' the children broke into groups for daily worship, with the Hindu assembly taking place in the school hall. State schools in England and Wales are able to secure a 'determination' in exceptional circumstances. This allows them to opt out of the mandate to provide collective worship of a 'broadly Christian character' as stated in the National Curriculum. In the case of this school, children and staff represented a number of different religious groups, the largest of which was Hindu.

Assemblies of other faith groups, including one described as 'secular' took place in classrooms. This practice ensured authentic religious observance, with staff not obliged to meet the national directive for Collective Worship. It also reduced the need for religious compromise; yet it seemed to promote division. The separation of children into assembly groups seemed to also be evident in the playground, inadvertently promoting a culture of suspicion. Prior to the session I asked one child if he thought it would be a good idea for the whole school to worship together. His response was as follows:

> It would be bad. There would be more arguments and fighting about who is right. In Muslim assembly we learn specific things from Mohammed and read the Qu'ran. We couldn't do this all together.

Therefore, the responses of the children following the research activity were significant for their social as well as their personal lives. The aim of the research was to ascertain the children's impressions of creating music in a collaborative situation. There was no religious intention behind the research questions; rather the project aimed to highlight the significance of music beyond the lesson plan. In order to be as neutral as possible, therefore providing the participants with a stimulus that was devoid of any prior meaning, I invited them to 'play a picture.' The picture in question was comprised of a number of shapes and patterns, painted with a range of shades of orange and yellow.

Choosing carefully which instrument might sound best, each child in a small group discussed, experimented and rehearsed their musical patterns. Together they created what they felt was a musical representation of the picture. The children clearly enjoyed the activity, and were proud of their work, each group performing to the rest of the class in turn.

The discussion that followed the activity was not only interesting, but transformative. Having been asked how they felt about working in a group, two children responded:

CHILD ONE: *It was fun, really playful, because everyone had to have a choice of instruments so everyone got to have a turn, so there was a bit of love in everybody.*

CHILD TWO: *Happy, because you hear all the other instruments. Excited, because there was loads of different instruments.*

The collaborative and enjoyable aspects of the music making are highlighted here. But more significantly, two further children made the following responses:

CHILD THREE: *When I am working with other people, like in this group, when I'm not playing with them in the playground, I am getting on with them better. They are like new friends.*

CHILD FOUR: *So, it makes me feel happy. When you're in the class, yeah, and on the playground, you only see your friends, so when you see them in a group and talk about music, we got to help each other.*

In terms of Bildung's Repetition, the Repetition aspect of this activity drew on the children's own history. In working together, and in the interplay promoted by the creative activity, they were able to recollect and reflect on the social divisions that had been constructed in their friendship groups; furthermore, they were able to evaluate how these had been eradicated in the process of creating the music. They were able to observe how they could work alongside children who are not usually part of their friendship group, and also consider them as new friends. In turn, in the informal conversation that took place following the session, some children commented on how they had enjoyed each other's company, and as a result would look to play with these children at lunchtime.

This is an example on a micro-scale of what might be termed inter-faith dialogue on a wider scale. The children articulated this act of solidarity as 'everyone worked together' and there was a strong sense that the children experienced 'oneness' in their music making. Here they recognised the need for staff and pupils of all religions to co-operate together, in 'an attempt to help people understand and accept the other in their otherness' (Ariarajah cited by Race 2001: 9). As Race notes (15), the children recognised that religious and cultural groups should not just tolerate each other, but should expand to encompass mutuality and share values in the search for new ways of understanding. The evidence from this school is that the acceptance of religions as relative truths engenders respect whilst affirming the beliefs of individuals and groups. Yet the music activity highlighted another value, that of 'dialogue, which assumes that there is truth on both sides, affirming maintaining and cherishing differences' (Knitter 1996: 24).

It is important to note that such an approach to inter-faith activity is supported and encouraged in my own context of the UK, where Religious Education is compulsory. A number of education systems are secular in nature, including those in Australia and France. Of Australia, Natsis writes: 'the current legislation for state schools is that they are secular' (2016: 69). It might be fair to say that religious visitors are treated with suspicion and religious activity is not encouraged. Other contexts such as the USA are not as explicitly prescriptive as the UK but whilst learning about religion is not prohibited, Religious Education should evidence a legitimate educational purpose.

On the other hand, countries in the Middle East, for example, find that their education systems are overtly religious, such as in Turkey where since 2002, the 'Islamist government has increased religious education (Sunni Islamic) at all levels, including early childhood education' (Kotaman 2018: 359). Therefore, religious and cultural sensitivity is required on the part of educators when considering such an open-ended perspective on learning. Inter-faith discussion and activity is not always appropriate or welcome; yet learners as human beings in their own existence world-over are able to bring themselves to any pedagogical situation and find meaning (Natasis, 74; Kotaman, 374).

In conclusion to this series of case studies then, it is possible to observe how a range of learning experiences led to reflections that had a deeper meaning to the learners than was prescribed or assessed by the session's learning objective. In some cases, the learning had a wider impact in that it determined a change of behaviour in the future, whilst being meaningful in the present. In every example, the existence of the learners was brought to the educational experience and inextricably linked to the process of learning. Being through Bildung was able to relate with the subject matter or class context in a movement of interplay. In the middle space between their Being and the context, the children were able to reflect on the meaning of the learning for the present, but as in Repetition, the learning in this moment was interrupted, preventing it from becoming standardised, and allowing it to be taken forward into the future.

In each case, cautions have been applied and reservations that teachers might have regarding this approach have been considered. Nevertheless, in reference to the notion of 'educare' revisited at the opening of this chapter, it might be argued that the 'drawing out' of learning that this term might encourage, not only had relevance for each individual learner but also for the school and wider community. If in addition to meeting the set requirements for each lesson, when children are given the opportunity to reflect and take their learning forward, this might have great consequences for the future. This chapter has prioritised formal areas of the curriculum in order to highlight to teachers how such an existential perspective might be acknowledged throughout the school day.

In a brief aside, it is important to highlight aspects of school life that do not comprise the formal curriculum but yet inspire learning such as that described here. One such aspect encouraged in my own school is the 'Eco-Schools' initiative.[6] In providing a space in which children are able to reflect on their understanding of the world, critique the behaviours of humans in relation to the planet and consider ways of making a difference, this valuable area of learning fully reflects the perspective that underpins Bildung's Repetition. In classes, the learning is pupil led and the activities provided are responsive to children's reflections.

In my own school context, one at a time, each child in a class takes home an eco-diary. This allows them to consider environmental issues as seen in everyday life, or in the media. They record their responses to these issues in the diary which are then shared with the class back in school. As there is no set objective, there is no interruption, but it is evident that in this case, the 'teacher' is not the adult at the front of the class, but the child who intervenes. The result of children's reflections and responses lead the way in inspiring class activity and to date, these have included tasks such as litter picking, planting seeds and creating a display wall full of recycled materials. A whole school recycling scheme has also emerged through the lessons. An eco-blog takes the learning forward, in order to share with parents and readers from the wider eco-community. The value of the blog is its opportunity for further responses and reflections, ensuring that learning does not remain in the enclosed space of the classroom but has a continual and evolving role in the ongoing environmental discourse.

A similar aspect, currently popular in the UK, is the Forest Schools[7] programme. Taking place outdoors, usually in the school's own natural environment, Forest Schools sessions, which again are pupil led and responsive to their ideas and reflections, involve children taking part in free or scaffolded play activities. They also participate in team-building activities or exploratory tasks such as den-building, making a fire, creating pictures with natural materials or setting their own trails and tracks. As much as adults are required for safety, health and hygiene, the children lead the learning, identifying the opportunities afforded by the natural environment and making suggestions for exploration. Again, the role of the adult 'teacher' in a formal sense is groundless, allowing the students to intervene with their own ideas. Often the result of such sessions is heightened self-esteem and confidence on the part of children, increased depth in relationships and a more tangible sense of trust between children and children, and between adults and children. This is not a top-down educational methodology, but in the light of the notion 'educare,' highlights the value of learner-led activity. In terms of Bildung's Repetition, Forest Schools evidence the transformational aspect of learning, which in the light of its three values 'inspiration, aspiration and transformation,' allows learning to be taken forward beyond the immediate, to facilitate long-lasting personal change.

A final aspect of non-curricular school life pertains to communal activity. There are many examples of such activity represented in primary schools; however, here I will focus on singing in a choir. As the subject leader for music in my school, I have always been involved in leading choir, advocating the value of singing in festivals, taking part in competitions or singing just for fun. Recently, the older children in school took part in a large-scale concert, involving over 100 school choirs, all singing together in a local arena.[8] A report on this concert was televised the following morning.[9] The television report included interviews with a small number of children who each gave their own responses regarding the value of the event. These responses included statements such as:

- We spread our talent
- We sang as one – we were all into the music
- I could be myself
- It shows I can do anything I put my mind to
- You gain confidence in yourself

Reflecting on Hyde's idea of 'ontological knowing' or on the concept of 'flow' introduced above, it is clear here that the act of communal singing had an existential impact on these children, and I dare say most children who took part. The responses are reminiscent of those from one of my own studies, undertaken in 2011. Having interviewed members of my school choir, inviting them to talk about their enjoyment of singing, their responses evidenced again examples of an existential dimension which had personal value to them (Wills 2011: 44). For example, one child remarked on gaining a sense of achievement:

> *I feel really good at choir and when we sing like at Christmas and in the hall. It makes me really happy. I like it when the teachers smile and tell us we have done well. It's like a feeling inside. You can feel it. It's the best thing in school.*

Another child remarked on how she had found her niche in school (44). One other referred to the corporeal nature of singing (45). Although she found it hard to articulate, she indicated that the vibrations made in the body when singing made her feel good. Another responded:

> It like gives you butterflies in your tummy. It jumps all over the place. I get excited and happy all the time.
>
> (45)

Again, the different kind of 'knowing' highlighted above is in evidence here; this resonates with what is referred to by Eugene Gendlin as the 'felt-sense.' He writes: 'No amount of symbols, definitions, and the like can be used in the place of the felt meaning' (1997: 5). Thus, this kind of knowing, surpassing representation, objectification and of course assessment is no less important to children, and as such must be recognised and valued as an integral part of education – not just an optional extra.

It is hoped that, whilst observing the cultural nuances of global contexts, the illustrations presented here might inspire all teachers who are required to deliver set curricula in a range of pedagogical situations. In the following chapter it will be illustrated how the philosophical perspective outlined in this book might be recognised in the classroom and adopted in wider school practice so that an existential dimension to education might not be feared or evaded, but embedded in daily practice.

Notes

1 https://en.wikipedia.org/wiki/And_Then_They_Came_for_Me accessed 4 April 2016.
2 www.gov.uk/dfe/nationalcurriculum accessed 22 November 2018.

3 See www.childrenspirituality.org/support/spirituality-days accessed 5 January 2019.
4 Differentiation in Primary Classrooms involves teachers providing children with different abilities with different tasks. This ensures that children all have the potential to succeed at their ability level.
5 The Fibonacci sequence involves finding a number by adding the two before it e.g. 1, 1, 2, 3, 5, 8, 13, 21 etc.
6 See Chapter 1, endnote 10.
7 www.forestschools.com 14 February 2019.
8 See www.youngvoices.co.uk 15 February 2019.
9 www.bbc.co.uk/newsround transmitted on 15 February 2019.

References

Adams, K., Hyde, B., and Woolley, R. (2008), *The Spiritual Dimension of Childhood*, London and Philadelphia: Jessica Kingsley Publishers.

Csikszentmihalyi, M. (1990), *Flow: The Psychology of Optimal Experience*, New York: Harper & Row.

Gendlin, E. (1997), *Experiencing and the Creation of Meaning*, Evanston, IL: Northwestern University Press.

Hay, D., and Nye, R. (2006), *The Spirit of the Child (Revised Edition)*, London: Jessica Kingsley Publishers.

Hyde, B. (2008), *Children and Spirituality: Searching for Meaning and Connectedness*, London and Philadelphia: Jessica Kingsley Publishers.

Knitter, P. (1996), *Jesus and the Other Names*, Oxford: Oneworld.

Kotaman, H. (2018), 'Comparison of impact of religious and secular education on young children's factuality judgments,' in *International Journal of Children's Spirituality*, 23, No. 4. 358–379.

McDowall Clark, R. (2016), *Childhood in Society for the Early Years*, London: SAGE.

Natsis, E. (2016), 'A new discourse on spirituality in public education. Confronting the challenges in a post-secular society,' in *International Journal of Children's Spirituality*, 21, No. 1. 66–77.

Race, A. (2001), *Interfaith Encounter*, London: SCM Press.

Watson, J. (2013), 'Knowing through the felt-sense: a gesture of openness to the other,' in *International Journal of Children's Spirituality*, 18, No. 1. 118–130.

Webster, R.S. (2004), 'An existential framework of spirituality,' in *International Journal of Children's Spirituality*, 9 No. 1. 7–19.

Wills, R. (2011), 'The Magic of Music: a study into the promotion of children's well-being through singing,' in *International Journal of Children's Spirituality*, 16, No. 1. 37–46.

5 Recommendations for policy and practice

Implications for education

The purpose of this final chapter is to provide a rationale for the book outside of academia. As much as it might provide a suitable text on a university reading list, without it influencing the thinking of those who set policy and determine what happens in practice, it will have limited value. Therefore, as the discussion concludes, ideas are proposed that might be adopted by those who hold the power in educational systems. Yet is also is relevant to teachers who are well established in their careers or are providers of Initial Teacher Training (ITT).

Throughout the propositions set out in this final chapter, it is important to have in mind the over-arching question *what is education*? As has been discussed already, it is proposed here that learning is about more than the acquisition of facts and skills. In the relation of self and other, learning as 'Bildung's Repetition' involves both the education of the self and the education of the school. The adult is not always the 'teacher' and indeed he or she might equally be a learner. Thus, this final chapter might be considered as a call for primary schools to develop critical thinkers, existentially aware learners, and human beings who can contribute to wider society and make a difference. This can only be done when education providers recognise and embrace the dimension of learning that goes beyond externally determined objectives, to encourage a wider understanding of what learning entails. It calls for a change in perspective on the part of Governments, Headteachers and classroom practitioners, and teacher educators. Each group will be addressed in turn.

Governments

In this section, is hoped that the influence of Bildung's Repetition might encourage those who make decisions about education to reflect existentially themselves on what education means beyond the constraints of tests and inspections.

At the time of writing, education in England is again in the news, as usual, for controversial reasons. Following the inspection of a number of 'Steiner Schools,' that is schools under Government jurisdiction but based on the principles of the Steiner-Waldorf movement, three in particular have recently been deemed to be failing, prompting the Chief Inspector of Schools and the Secretary of State for Education to undertake a substantial review of all schools led under the Steiner philosophy. The accusations made against these schools pertained to their failure to 'meet the standards' required for learning and safeguarding;[1] yet it must be noted that the standards required, set by the current and previous Government, are not in line with Steiner ideology. It is difficult to equate Steiner education, which delays formal educational activities until at least age seven, and which prioritises outdoor and experiential learning, with school standards that are driven by values that are tangentially different.

In this situation, the judgements of the inspection body incited outrage on the part of parents. Families involved with the schools in question signed petitions and raised money to campaign against the findings of the reports and to retain the Steiner ethos in their respective contexts. In fact, the campaign group working on behalf of one of the schools gained a substantial number of signatures in favour of adopting Steiner principles across *all* schools. According to parents, 'The Steiner approach to learning promotes good mental health among children' and as teachers 'give as much focus to children's spiritual, emotional and creative development as their ability to master the three Rs,' it is believed that such an holistic approach is necessary for children's well-being and self-esteem.[2] In an era when mental health in children is a growing concern, it seems ironic that an approach to education which seems to foster positive mental health is being brought under such negative scrutiny.

In promoting learning beyond the objective in all primary schools, I suggest therefore that Governments might recognise the value that practitioners in Steiner schools and others led on similar principles have, in order to allow for the creative space that encourages children to invest in their own learning and the development of the learning of others. Furthermore, looking back to the principles of the early pioneers in education might allow a return to an understanding of the etymology of the word 'education' so to consider how learning might once again involve a process of drawing out rather than being drawn towards targets and standards.

As Steiner schools seem to place a priority on different aspects of education than those deemed to be acceptable for 'meeting the standards,' the educational experiences they provide are diametrically opposed to the latest initiative from the Department for Education, which is the testing of children aged four in Mathematics and English. This initiative is to be trialled in primary schools from September 2019. In contrast to children in countries such as Austria, Croatia and Bulgaria (McDowall Clark 2016: 43), as well as Steiner schools, whose induction to formal education is delayed until age six or seven, the pendulum in England has swung the other way – the emphasis now on assessing numeracy and literacy being a present factor in school from the outset. In the Early Years Foundation Stage, whose guidelines have a strong emphasis on child development through play, experiential learning and child agency, it is likely that these favourable aspects of learning will be relegated to second place in favour of the curriculum areas to be tested.

This raises concerns regarding teacher workload and pupil stress. Highlighted by Nancy Stewart from the Association for Professional Development in the Early Years:

> the baseline test will bring extra workload for teachers, as well as stress for children right at the start of their school experience when settling in happily and confidently should have first priority. And they will bring pressure to focus relentlessly on narrow skills from the moment these very young children enter the school gates.[3]

Such a directive towards schooling is antithetical to the values of holistic and experiential learning that historically have shaped nurseries, infant schools and other early years settings. From a Scottish perspective, Liz Smith, education spokesperson for the Scottish Conservative Party argues:

> Froebel did not ask infant teachers to make use of standardised tests or assessments. Instead, he asked them to be skilled in their professional judgements and well-informed, through daily observation of each child, which would then be discussed with each family.[4]

It might be suggested then that the prioritising of testing and assessing is detrimental not only to well-being but also to learning.

This idea is in evidence in the experiences of children at the other end of the age spectrum, that is in the first years of High School (aged 11+), in countries such as Finland, Denmark and Sweden. In their 2014 journal article, Heta Tuominen-Soini and Katariina Salmela-Aro argue that a high-stakes testing school environment can lead to what they term 'burnout.' Burnout is evidenced by low level engagement in learning and a loss of interest in school-work. Part of the problem as they see it is that schools are failing to establish environments in which students can flourish. Rather, 'high teacher expectations, less caring and supportive teacher–student relationships, and increasing social comparisons and competition experienced by those on the academic track might contribute to creating a misfit between the student and the educational environment' (2014: 651). What their research study identifies is a clear correlation between student stress and symptoms of depression with a fear of failure, as well as noting that those who achieve less well evidence lower self-esteem (655). Both aspects are influenced by 'demanding school tasks' and their pre-occupation with success and performance, rather than valuing the whole school experience (659).

Widening to consider the impact of inspections on schools, Ehren, Perryman and Shackleton observe how the inspection framework in the Netherlands actually has little impact on the wider school experience. Whilst acknowledging that 'in Europe, the dominant arrangement for educational accountability is school inspections' (2015: 296), they raise questions regarding the significance of such scrutiny, suggesting that schools improve best when responding to 'indirect developmental processes rather than through more direct coercive methods, such as schools accepting inspection feedback' (297). They also note that when schools are more responsive to inspection feedback, 'new teaching approaches and curriculum experimentation may not occur as the school focuses instead on meeting the expected inspection standards. This links to the concepts of performativity and gaming' (297).

This notion of 'playing the game' is reflected in that of 'teaching to the test,' which has been evaluated in the teacher practice of schools in the USA. As introduced in Chapter 1, the *No Child left Behind* programme in American state schools, requires the standardised testing of children in Grades Three to Eight (aged 8+). According to Jennings and Bearak (2014), the benefits of perceived increased pupil attainment in the NCLB era, must be weighed against the quality of teaching that children might receive if the pressure of tests was removed. They posit that the inflation of scores in primary school classrooms is in some part due to the act of 'teaching to the test,' which not only includes directed subject and skill-based learning but also a strong emphasis on recognising and responding positively to the structure of test papers, and the student's ability to navigate their way through the questions. This changes the focus of education away from what the children have learnt, to how skilled they are in taking tests. They write:

> The experiential costs and benefits of teaching to the test must be assessed against the counterfactual of what would be happening in a given classroom in the absence of the pressures associated with the state test. As a result, teaching to the test has different costs and benefits across different classrooms and schools. It is in those classrooms where the counterfactual educational experience is rich and of high quality that teaching to the test potentially has the largest negative impacts.
>
> (2014: 382)

In promoting learning beyond the objective in all primary schools, I suggest therefore that Governments might accept the detrimental effect that testing has on both on the mental and emotional lives of learners and teachers, and recognise that in meeting the standards and targets set nationally, practitioners will be inclined to prioritise subjects and teaching methods that promote good results. Furthermore, in relegating the status of arts-based subjects, as well as others that are not measured, that often encourage connectedness, fulfilment and self-esteem, the opportunities for social development and teamwork are reduced. As it is often these open-ended activities that promote learning beyond the objective, I propose that the balance be redressed, with less emphasis on measuring progress, and more given to the development of learners as human beings.

In addition to formal research such as the studies highlighted here, looking at anecdotal evidence from a range website stories and online videos,[5] it is clear that the desire for a rich and quality school experience, as suggested in the quote above, is the priority for many parents. This desire is reflected in the rhetoric of teaching unions and petitioning bodies that are currently campaigning for a systematic change. The over-riding concern is that those in national leadership do not seem to understand that there is that there is more to the primary school experience than high attainment on tests. Reflecting the discussion in earlier chapters of this book, the influence of external drivers on teacher-practice and school improvement seem to bypass the learners as individuals. As the homepage of a petitioning website states:

> Primary school children in England are among the most tested in the world. They're used as data points in a system which damages

their education and benefits no-one. We believe they deserve better. We want pupils to enjoy a rich and varied curriculum and leave primary school with a love of learning, instead of spending months preparing for tests in English and maths. We support teachers who want to spend their time stimulating young minds and expanding pupils' knowledge and creative problem-solving skills, not 'teaching to the test.' We believe schools should be judged on the overall quality of education they provide, not the results of a narrow set of standardised tests.

(www.morethanascore.org.uk)

Reflecting on recent news from New Zealand, where the new Labour Government has overturned the paradigm of testing, it seems that children in primary schools are more able to flourish and thrive without the external drivers for success. According to Paul Goulter, General Secretary of NZEI Union for Primary Head and Staff, the ineffective linear method of teaching and assessment has been replaced by one that is more akin to children – 'up and down!' He notes that in creating a political space for conversation (about the nature of education in the next 30 years), including parents, teachers, students and teaching unions, teaching methods 'rooted in a broad and rich curriculum' might become the priority, in relation with assessment processes that are more compatible with where children are at.[6]

I suggest in promoting learning beyond the objective in all primary schools, that Governments might consider allowing children to learn 'without limits' (using the rhetoric of Paul Goulter). If the priority of accountability through testing and inspections was lessened, this might allow practitioners to embrace the existential dimension of learning without fear of failure or scrutiny. If the nonlinear aspect of children's lives was embraced, so that learners are not considered one-size-fits-all, it might mean that their experience of school could prepare them to become critical and responsible citizens, with the potential for creativity and problem-solving unleashed. If the demands of the curriculum were also lessened, with reduced emphasis on knowledge and more on experience, and if Governments were to provide schools with more time in which children could reflect on learning and respond, schooling might inspire learners in their own Being to become individuals and groups who affect social, political and environmental change.

It might seem that my suggestions are slightly verbose. I do not intend the result of adopting my perspective to be game-changing for education and society. It is also important to note again that the aim of this book is not to overturn the paradigm of education as we know it in the wider global context (although from the example of New Zealand, it is evident that campaigning and the rejection of Government requirements *can* result in an overturning). What I am calling for is a change in perspective – regarding the status of children as learners (or teachers) and what education is for – on the part of those who make the ultimate decisions.

This will require a letting go of the stronghold of performativity, which involves economic as well as educational factors, and the allowance of a substantial enough change to affect the experience of learners in the primary school classroom–yet without negating the curriculum or eroding standards. The case studies presented in this book illustrate how this is possible. As I have posited above, this change requires not a whole paradigm shift, but a ten-degree movement in perspective. As the philosophical perspective of Bildung's Repetition encourages the opening of a critical space in classrooms, it is hoped that this book might in turn encourage the opening of a critical space in Parliament and Government offices worldwide, so to inspire politicians and educational ministers to recognise the value of existence above and beyond what might be measured and assessed.

School leaders and teachers

In 2004, I attended the International Conference on Children's Spirituality, held in Lincoln, UK. Brendan Hyde, an Australian scholar cited several times in this book, presented a paper, which having subsequently been published, inspired my practice both as a philosopher and as a classroom teacher. In his observation of a primary school classroom in Melbourne, children aged ten read a story from the indigenous Aboriginal culture. The story involved familiar characters from the Dreamtime stories and the children engaged with it 'logically and rationally' (2005: 32). However, an interruption to this accepted form of learning came in the response of a child (pseudonym David), who thoughtfully and reflectively uttered: 'It is beyond logic.' This declaration, according to Hyde signalled an awareness on the part of the child that the story might inspire another dimension of enquiry – in this case the realm of mystery. Unfortunately, in this scenario the class teacher directed the discussion away from this response, resulting in what Hyde determines as 'a lost opportunity' (32). However, he writes: 'perhaps there was a sense in which David's comment indicated that not everything is governed by logic and rationalism' (32).

In reflecting philosophically on this situation, Hyde notes that what is important in education is the middle space between the learner and 'text.' Reminiscent of the interplay of Bildung, he likens the process of learning that takes place in this space to play. Thus, it is important for practitioners to understand children's awareness beyond the immediate and take seriously 'the challenge to enter the middle space that is opened up in a playful and dialogical engagement' (Hyde 2005: 35). It is equally important for practitioners to take seriously those moments in which children might interrupt the current state of Being, to take the learning into 'an alternative way of being in the world' (42). Hyde suggests that moments such as this, whilst not planned for, do occur frequently in classroom contexts. The response of the teacher then, should be to be open and responsive to such moments: to 'encourage learners to think more deeply in this way' (42). A significant aspect of my own ethos as a teacher was subsequently influenced by this story, and in the years that have followed, it has been my aim to avoid any lost opportunities. I have always endeavoured to embrace such moments as special and sacred.

I suggest that in promoting learning beyond the objective in all primary schools, teachers might embrace the moments in which learner's thoughts and personal responses take them away from the present, to allow for the consideration of something deeper and more meaningful. Of course, lessons always have expected outcomes with objectives to meet. Teachers are also very busy and are constantly aware of the pressures to provide a full curriculum. Yet as Hyde's observations, and the case studies outlined in this book suggest, if a teacher is willing to become aware of that which is beyond the objective in the thinking of certain children, it might just change one individual's engagement in class, influence his or her self-esteem and lead the way towards further and deeper learning.

The notion of the middle space as described here is a feature of Bildung's Repetition. It involves recognising the space between self and other that allows for creative interplay and the inspiration of new meanings. Of course, the space in this pedagogical perspective is a philosophical space which is unseen. However, the notion of space might also be considered in terms of the classroom, the school day and wider school organisation. Jack Miller, a Canadian scholar, has written extensively about holistic education. Without being overtly religious, his text *Education and the Soul* (2000), considers how a child-centred approach might promote authentic learning. In the forward to this text, Thomas Merton highlights that education 'is not the same as teaching' (2000: vii). He furthermore argues that when a learner's 'innate being is led out' (vii), learning 'makes the shift from mind to soul' (viii), and as such he declares that education becomes less about conformity and more about the individual child (viii).

As the discussion proceeds, Miller provides a plethora of ideas, with philosophical underpinning, as to how this might be made manifest in practice. In terms of providing space, he suggests that classrooms become like a sanctuary, the characteristics of which include acknowledging learner's feelings, validating children's selves, and experiencing community. Miller points out that there is no recipe for the sanctuary, and akin to my own assertions which note that Bildung's Repetition cannot be applied, but rather recognised, he avoids providing suggestions. His argument is against collecting tools, for practice, preferring instead to instil values (2000: vii, 9–10). However, some important principles are outlined which I think are relevant to this discussion.

First, for teachers to be aware of the awareness of children, they must be similarly aware of their own potentiality for Being. This self-awareness opens up the ability to be present, and therefore to be more tuned in to those moments in which children respond to learning beyond the immediate. Times of quiet or silence at various points during the school day allow children to focus on what might be stirring in their thoughts or imaginations (Miller 2000: 110). Playing music, reading poetry and telling stories all provide opportunities for interaction in the middle space (111), and rituals (such as singing every morning, or having quiet time before lunch) can afford the opportunity for children to slow down, feel safe, and express themselves in a context of trust (112). Finally, Miller proposes that schools might include 'nourishing voice' (112). He writes: 'of course, the leaders in our schools must be comfortable cultivating an environment where voice can be heard.' Nevertheless, he suggests: 'each person needs to ask himself or herself where am I speaking from? Am I speaking mostly from my head or from the deeper part of myself?' (112).

I suggest that in promoting learning beyond the objective in all primary schools, teachers might spend a moment to pause and consider their own identity as an existential Being. When a teacher is present to him or herself, the potential for presence and therefore meaningful moments is enhanced. I also suggest that the classroom might be viewed as more than a physical space. In the rhetoric of Sue Philips, the classroom can become a 'theatre of learning' (2003: 55–66). As such the classroom provides the condition in which children's imaginations might be arrested or stirred, and in addition to the affective dimension of learning, it can also be a safe space of trust, empathy, mutual understanding and compassion. Multi-sensory approaches, as well as silence and ritual might facilitate this, encouraging children and adults alike to be present to each other.

It might be argued by the majority involved in teaching that education is adult-centric. Adults make decisions or demands on behalf of children, but rarely involve them in policy making or lesson planning. As much as child agency is a key feature of the Early Years Foundation Stage Profile, with children's interests and ideas enabling personalised learning, in the subsequent years of primary school this is eroded. Nevertheless, one of the interesting features of the case studies presented in the previous chapter is that it was the children who instigated the learning that went beyond the objective. The final stage of Bildung's Repetition is the interruption and inspiration for future conduct, and in each case study, it was the children that interrupted the learning that developed in the middle space. Therefore, in considering how an existential perspective on learning might be promoted in schools, it might be pertinent to involve children in the decision making – to allow them to become the interruption that disallows the ideas of politicians or parents to be claimed as truth, and to become the searchlight that illuminates the inadequacies of the dichotomy.

Again, this will require practitioners to release the stronghold of performativity, and to embrace the risk that comes with accepting groundlessness. When the 'teacher,' be it adult or child intervenes, mastery becomes groundless. Yet this provides the condition through which the loss of power opens up new possibilities for a revised perspective on thinking and learning. Over and above any theorising on my part, or the presentation of ideas as posed here, it is the voices of the children that I believe will motivate those in leadership to consider a new perspective.

Listening to children has been encouraged over recent years, in particular in the creation of school councils and children's parliaments. Currently the notion of pupil voice,[7] is actively promoted in UK primary schools. Pupil voice involves children offering their opinions and ideas regarding their school experience. It encourages child participation in establishing and developing a school's ethos and aids school improvement by inviting children to identify future priorities.

Pupil voice allows children to share their views on their school experience and offer suggestions for change. These ideas are of course welcome. However, in my thinking, learning beyond the objective involves more than the sharing of opinions. When children are given the opportunity to bring their existence and experiences to learning, and allowed to reflect and share, the outcome is much more profound.

As illustrated through the responses of the children to learning about Civil Rights, as described in Chapter 4, what the children gained from the reflection and interruption was a call to change. In conclusion to this evaluation of the role of teachers, I urge those in authority to listen to children – not just to listen to their opinions, but to what it happening in their lives on a much deeper level. It might just change the world.

According to Nigel Tubbs, and as has been noted in earlier chapters, the interruption not only prevents education from becoming fixed and perpetuated as truth, it also throws into question who the teacher might be. In reference to the indirect methods of writing adopted by Kierkegaard, he suggests that it is indirect learning that has true meaning (2005: 224). Therefore, what is learnt through the interplay of Bildung becomes authentic to each learner. However, by now it is clear that Bildung per se is inadequate. Tubbs notes how for Kierkegaard subjective knowledge, 'generated inwardly by experience' (224) becomes a universality in its own terms (225). What is needed is a teacher to bring the truth to the learning situation, and take it forward to the future. This teacher is the third partner in learning, and as the interruption, promotes the negation of the negation (226). In practical terms, this means that the 'teacher,' who intervenes to take the learning beyond the objective, not only negates the formal aims of the lesson but also negates that which is drawn out from within. In Hyde's case study, the child known as David indeed interrupted the literacy lesson. Yet, unfortunately, he was denied the opportunity to become the 'teacher,' thus disallowing existential learning from taking place and potentially discouraging him from being so open in the future.

I suggest in promoting learning beyond the objective in all primary schools, that teachers might consider how valuable the voice of children can be, over and above expressing their opinions. Allowing learners to take control as it were, is risky. Not only is the outcome of engaging in learning in such a way unknown, it also poses a risk to the authority of classroom practitioners. However, in negating the negation, Bildung's Repetition does not seek to overturn the authority of those trained to be in charge of classes. What it does however is open up the potential for children to contribute to learning from their own perspectives, so to widen the dimension of classroom experience and ground education in their existence as learning Beings.

Initial teacher training

In January 2019, the UK's Department for Education published supporting advice and criteria for institutions who provide ITT. These guidelines suggest that providers should offer specialist subject knowledge as well as training in pedagogy to enable them to teach across their chosen age range. The suggested content of programmes delivered to student teachers is quite pragmatic and in keeping with the observations made in this book, the topics suggested are heavily focused on planning and assessment. Further topics include important issues such as dealing with behaviour, child development and learning, as well as attention to education for children with special needs and disabilities.[8]

In consideration of these guidelines, two details seem to command some attention. The first topic suggested in the guidelines for ITT institutions refers to the 'role of the teacher.' It is difficult to locate any literature from the Department for Education that unpacks this further, therefore how this subject is approached will be specific to each provider. However, it seems that an exploration of what it means to be a teacher provides an opportunity for students to consider the existential dimension of education, and how an understanding of who *they are* in their Being might encourage *learners* in their Being. This calls for an engagement with Philosophy of Education. This does not suggest that student teachers embark on an exegesis of texts in the canon of western philosophy, but rather that they might reflect philosophically on the meaning of their Being as teacher within an understanding of what an existential dimension of learning might be.

In the book *New Perspectives in Philosophy of Education*, David Lundie highlights the role of Information Technology in Higher Education. In principle, he considers the aim of such education as developing conscious subjects, in contrast to the development of any subject knowledge base (2014: 52). It is the teacher in his or her 'myness' that directs the path of learning (53). Yet when reflecting further, Lundie suggests that such human ontology 'is augmented by information and communication technologies' (54). Thus, the student is not a law unto his or herself, but is involved in community.

In many Higher Education Institutions worldwide, online forums, learning networks and the like are now a key feature of the learning experience, with the aim of creating such community and allowing for discussion and the development of thinking in a creative space. Lundie argues however that in such forums there is the potential for learning and evaluation to 'collapse into one another' (2014: 53) when the critical dimension of the space and learner agency begin 'to be elided' (53). What is important then is an understanding of the Being of the teacher as learner, but within a critical community.

I suggest in promoting learning beyond the objective in ITT, it is imperative, in the light of the topic 'the role of the teacher' to bring to the fore the critical question of who the teacher might be. If the teacher in the experience of ITT is not only the individual hired to scaffold the subject development of the trainee, but extends to being represented by other students in a learning network, or even the self, some attention to who the teacher in a primary school classroom 'is' will be valuable. This is a philosophical issue, which highlights the necessity of philosophy in ITT, not only in grounding education in an historical philosophical context, but in the developing of forums that facilitate critical thinking. Furthermore, an understanding of who the teacher in his or her 'myness' is important to cultivate, as well as promoting an awareness of how this 'myness' as Being, might be understood in terms of the Being-in-the-world of all participants in classroom learning.

The second detail that commands attention pertains to pedagogy. Documentation on ITT refers to subject-based pedagogy and the need for trainee teachers to have an understanding of 'related pedagogy' (see Endnote 8). However, according to Tony Eaude in his text *How do Expert Classroom Teachers really work?* there exists a suspicion of pedagogy not only amongst student teachers but in schools in general. The problem as he sees it is that 'most teachers in primary schools have come to accept being told how to teach, with a prescribed model based on simple and largely non-negotiable guidance, with a strong emphasis on content and outcomes in literacy and numeracy' (2012: 2). When understanding pedagogy involves developing knowledge of learning and teaching methods, including philosophies of education and educational theory, it must be acknowledged that amongst the many demands placed on student teachers, this becomes relegated to an optional extra. Concurring with Eaude's assertion about teacher training currently responding to prescribed outcomes, and in the light of my own experience, I posit that the paradigm of school-based teacher training which is a growing concern in the UK, actually is a philosophical concern.

As outlined above, the main components of ITT are pragmatic and practical. As such they provide prospective teachers with the tools they will require for the classroom. Of course, each tool is important particularly when concerned with behaviour management, planning, differentiation and assessment. In a sense they comprise the teacher's survival kit. Furthermore, when students are mainly school-based, their success often relates to the practice of teaching as provided by the school context of which they are a part. Yet it might be argued that each tool reflects something of the immediate in learning. Each can be measured and evaluated, observed and assessed. But without a deeper understanding of what effective teaching entails, of who the teacher might be and recognition of the existential dimension of

learning, students become curriculum deliverers rather than pedagogues. Between the two is a fundamental difference.

The difference highlights the gap between the view of education outlined in Chapter 1, which might be described as the performativity discourse, and the view of education that recognises more than what can
be measured. In an article by Burn and Mutton, published online in
2018 for the *Journal of the Chartered College of Teaching*,[9] it is observed
that criticality and the analytical dimension of teacher's thinking is suspended in teacher education until practitioners have fully undertaken
their training and started out on their teaching careers. Teacher training
then, rather than providing the critical creative space encouraged by
Lundie and Eaude, becomes another means to end exercise. This results
in practitioners who are able to meet performance criteria but might not
fully understand what teaching is. The authors of this article draw on research from Winch, Oancea and Orchard (2015: 202–216) who describe
such teachers as craft workers or executive technicians, with the 'job
description' of each, inadequate for the wider role of teacher.

According to Eaude, an expert teacher is the practitioner who not
only provides the critical space but also creates the right climate and
context for trans-technical teaching and learning (2012: 24). This involves encouraging student teachers to consider not only what they do
but how they do it (26). The author provides a helpful checklist that is
useful here (27):

- Observe carefully
- Listen attentively
- Talk sparingly
- Explain clearly
- Question insightfully
- Wait patiently
- Respond thoughtfully
- Challenge gently

Therefore, I suggest in promoting learning beyond the objective in
ITT, it is important that programmes include training not only on how
to provide, assess and evaluate learning experiences but also include
sessions what teaching means. It is also important that teacher educators consider how students of ITT might become reflective and critical
pedagogues. In so doing, it might be possible to create a culture and
climate in the classroom that allows for personal response, is safe, and
is accepting of the ontological differences that children bring to each
learning experience.

Finally, it is necessary to consider the role of Spiritual, Moral, Social and Cultural education in ITT. Being known in the UK by its acronym SMSC, this aspect of school life might be equated to programmes such as *Values Education* in Australia[10] as well as the *Character and Moral Education* of a Singapore context[11] The 2013 publication by Adams, Monahan and Wills, 'Losing the whole child? A national survey of primary education training provision for Spiritual, Moral, Social and Cultural development,' identified how students across the UK experienced a varying quality and quantity of training in SMSC. Whilst evidence from Welsh ITT providers suggested a robust engagement with the subject, other English and Scottish institutions seemed to provide little amount of time on the subject – ranging from one hour to two days provision (2015: 205).

The value of SMSC in the opinion of the authors is its allusion to a more holistic dimension of learning, in contrast with the more performative aspects outlined here. Several participants in the research project, all teacher educators, recognised the value of the subject. One described it as being more than a subject stating: 'I think it is vital student teachers begin to understand SMSC because it underpins their whole educational philosophy in school' (2013: 209). Others noted the impact of the subject on self -esteem and confidence, community cohesion, and in engendering respect (209). From a philosophical perspective, and in line with the current discussion, it was noted that the subject has an implication on children's recognition of themselves as Beings in their own contingent identities, and as becomings in their potential for participation in society (209).

Yet the research data featured in this article suggests that the subject, whilst being a legal requirement in schools, is undervalued in ITT. The politics of macro-level influence is deemed as a significant factor, with one university lecturer observing that time spent on SMSC was decreased due to:

> ...external pressure on ITT to demonstrate impact in high-priority subject teaching such as phonics. I worry for the future of SMSC in both schools and ITT in this context.
>
> (2013: 208)

In addition, other respondents 'perceived that the importance afforded to subjects such as phonics, literacy more widely, and numeracy superseded the importance of SMSC' (208). Re-iterating the point cited by Eaude above, participants lamented the reduction in value of the more existential dimension of SMSC, rather noting that evaluating the inclusion of the subject across the curriculum represents not much more than a box ticking exercise (208–209).

In promoting learning beyond the objective in ITT, I therefore request that the less technocratic elements of the student experience are not minimised. As suggested above, the dimensions of education such as the cultural and social take learning away from being an individualistic enterprise towards embracing 'other' in a variety of senses. Cross- and inter-cultural practice inspires not just mutuality but a sense of interdependence and responsibility, whilst engaging in social action provides the opportunity for critical reflection on one's own lifestyle, often prompting change. The spiritual and moral aspects again lead learners beyond the immediate, often in reflection and critical thinking; thus, encouraging student teachers to develop an appreciation of the wider aspects of children's lives, might open up for them the middle space in which they too might reflect on their position and practice in the classroom.

In conclusion to this chapter, I propose then that participants in education, on a range of levels, might consider the value of what is described here as 'learning beyond the objective.' In adopting a slight change in perspective, the experience of children in primary schools might become more holistic, personal and meaningful. Without negating the curriculum or learning objectives, the existential dimension of learning might highlight what is 'really' being learnt, and in inviting the interruption of immediacy, introducing the teacher in another form, learning-led education might change the way children experience school for the better.

Afterword

It is important to acknowledge that further and more robust empirical research is required in order to evidence the benefits of this perspective to for attainment, mental health and learner attitude. It remains to be seen what the long-term impact of Bildung's Repetition might have on school life. As much of the material presented here pertains to personal reflections on practice as well as small scale research projects, the assertions of this book are located in my own philosophical and educational world. Furthermore, it is impossible to assess or quantify the life-long impact that the learning in the case studies presented here had on the children, and indeed if it had any impact beyond the one significant moment.

Nevertheless, as a philosophical practitioner, I encourage readers to 'let go' of what they already know so to think beyond legal requirements, and consider the Being of all involved in school – adults and children alike. I also encourage readers to embrace the risk and groundlessness that accompanies this letting go. I hope that the classroom teachers who struggle with the tension between attending to children's lives and working with them to attain set goals might learn to embrace the broken relation between the two as an ethical expression of authentic learning, and to accept that it is the learning that takes place in the middle space (of the tension) that is most significant. Finally, I encourage all partners in education to view classrooms as not only the space for achievement but the condition for meaningful and transformative education. In a new perspective on teaching and learning, looking out for what happens beyond the objective might be a good place to start.

Notes

1 Letter to Amanda Spielman from Damian Hinds. https://assets.publishing. service.gov.uk/government/uploads/system/uploads/attachment_data/ file/775293/HMCI_Steiner_Schools_letter_response.pdf accessed 7 February 2019.
2 https://www.independent.co.uk/news/education/education-news/parents-steiner-schools-ofsted-academy-bristol-exeter-legal-action-petition-education-a8764651.html accessed 7 February 2019.
3 https://www.morethanascore.org.uk/2019/01/16/baseline-assessment-out-of-the-frying-pan-into-the-fire/ accessed 7 February 2019.
4 https://www.gov.scot/publications/literature-review-teacher-education-21st-century/pages/6/ accessed 7 February 2019.
5 See for example www.neu.org.uk and www.morethanascore.org.uk both accessed 7 February 2019.
6 https://www.morethanascore.org.uk/2019/01/06/new-zealand-stopped-standardised-testing/ accessed 7 February 2019.
7 See https://www.estyn.gov.wales/news/%E2%80%98pupil-voice%E2%80%99-benefits-pupils-and-helps-schools-improve accessed 22 February 2019.
8 https://www.gov.uk/government/publications/initial-teacher-training-criteria/initial-teacher-training-itt-criteria-and-supporting-advice accessed 18 January 2019.
9 https://impact.chartered.college/article/constructing-curriculum-initial-teacher-education-when-new-teachers-encouraged-ask-critical-questions/ accessed 11 February 2019.
10 http://www.curriculum.edu.au/values/values_homepage,8655.html accessed 11 February 2019.
11 https://www.moe.gov.sg/docs/default-source/document/education/sylla-buses/character-citizenship-education/files/character-and-citizenship-education-(primary)-syllabus-(english).pdf accessed 11 February 2019.

References

Adams, K., Monahan, J., and Wills, R. (2015), 'Losing the whole child? A national survey of primary education training provision for spiritual, moral, social and cultural development,' in *European Journal of Teacher Education*, 38, No. 2. 199–216.

Eaude, T. (2012), *How do Expert Classroom Teachers Really Work?* London: Critical Publishing Limited.

Ehren, M., Perryman, J., and Shackleton, N. (2015), 'Setting expectations for Good Education: how Dutch School Inspections drive improvement,' in *School Effectiveness and School Improvement*, 26, No. 2. 1–32.

Hyde, B. (2005), 'Beyond logic – entering the realm of mystery: hermeneutic phenomenology as a tool for reflecting on children's spirituality,' in *International Journal of Children's Spirituality*, 10, No. 1. 31–44.

Jennings, J., and Bearak, J. (2014), 'Teaching to the test in the NCLB era: how test predictability affects our understanding of student performance,' in *Educational Researcher*, 48, No. 8. 381–389.

Lundie, D. (2014), 'Learning analytics and the education of the human,' in Lewin, D., Guilherme, A. and White, M. (eds), *New Perspectives on Philosophy of Education*, London: Bloomsbury Academic.

McDowall Clark, R. (2016), *Childhood in Society for the Early Years*, London: Sage Publications Limited.

Merton, T. (2000), 'Forward,' in Miller, J. (ed.), *Education and Soul*, Albany: State University of New York Press.

Miller, J. (2000), *Education and Soul*, Albany: State University of New York Press.

Philips, S. (2003), 'Reflections on classroom practice: the theatre of learning,' in *International Journal of Children's Spirituality*, 8, No. 1. 55–66.

Tubbs, N. (2005), *The Philosophy of the Teacher*, Oxford: Blackwell.

Tuominen-Soini, H., and Salmela-Aro, K. (2014), 'Schoolwork engagement and burnout among finnish high school students and young adults: profiles, progressions, and educational outcomes,' in *Developmental Psychology*, 50, No. 3. 649–662.

Winch, C., Oancea, A., and Orchard, J. (2015), 'The contribution of educational research to teacher's professional learning: philosophical understandings,' in *Oxford Review of Education*, 41, No. 2. 202–216.

Index

Note: Page numbers followed by "n" denote endnotes.